D1389051

SCOOPS

SCOOPS

Behind the Scenes of the BBC's
Most Shocking Interviews

SAM McALISTER

ONEWORLD

A Oneworld Book

First published by Oneworld Publications in 2022

ISBN 978-0-86154-440-0
eISBN 978-0-86154-441-7

Typeset by Hewer Text UK Ltd, Edinburgh
Printed and bound in Great Britain by Clays Ltd, Elcograf S.p.A.

Oneworld Publications
10 Bloomsbury Street
London WC1B 3SR
England

Stay up to date with the latest books,
special offers, and exclusive content from
Oneworld with our newsletter

Sign up on our website
oneworld-publications.com

To my beautiful, clever, charismatic and resilient mum, Netta, who taught me to mix with princes and paupers, but probably didn't mean it literally. And to Lucas, the best kid in the world.

CONTENTS

INTRODUCTION

Relentless. I've heard this word a lot. It's a moniker of admiration, confusion, and sometimes of abuse or ridicule. And it perfectly sums up who I am and what I do.

I'm not sure when or how it started but I live to 'get the story', to beat the world's media, to go first and, preferably, exclusively. News takes many forms and I don't discriminate – I've tracked down world leaders for their first interviews on the job, those on the brink of reputational ruin, and people who have everything, maybe even their life, to lose. Over the years, the desire to win has only grown. It has crept into every dinner, every party, every new acquaintance, every relationship, every business meeting. Every single encounter would allow me to build a crucial network – to get myself into a position where I, someone who arrived in journalism with no connections, no credentials and, dare I say, no credibility, could access virtually anyone in the world.

My path to news addiction wasn't a traditional one. News and politics weren't a feature of my childhood. In fact, they barely figured at all. We lived an itinerant life. My dad, who had made some money selling mobile homes, left the UK in the 1970s, moving my mum and me from tax haven to tax haven. Not the glamorous kind, like Monaco or the British Virgin Islands. Instead, he relocated us from the outskirts of London to Guernsey (so small I often felt I might fall off) and then to the Isle of Man (a cruel fate for any teen) and, finally, a short sojourn in Andorra (a flat perched in the mountains of a ski resort for three people who had never skied). These places shared something else in common – they didn't see themselves as part of their parent countries.

Each small island or municipality had a certain autonomy over several aspects of its political, fiscal and social affairs – and so you would have a feeling of belonging to something quite separate, figuratively and literally, from the larger powers just a few miles away. Usually, and quite understandably, the locals would, at best, tolerate or, at worst, actively detest the tax tourists who populated their small slice of the planet, filling their natural beauty with oversized cars and fragile egos. Of course, I knew I was

British, but my concerns were with small island life. People were much more likely to be discussing matters that affected them close to home – the cost of living, local services, neighbourhood gossip – than the kind of big social and political issues that came to fill my later years. I knew there was a bigger world out there, but it felt entirely irrelevant to my existence. We left our cars and houses unlocked, children could amble to school alone, no one had ever been murdered, no one had ever been raped, there were no burglaries. Shoplifting and traffic infractions were about as thrilling as it got. Occasionally a sheep might mosey into the garden looking for excitement or, more likely, some fresh grass. Days merged into years easily and without incident. It was a time without pandemics, without terror attacks, without war. I rode my bike, climbed rocks, swam and revelled in the pleasures that island life can bring.

There was no pressure to 'achieve' in the traditional way that so many middle-class kids seem to feel. My parents only expected me home on time and to be well mannered. My mum, a charismatic and beautiful woman, full of backbone and charm, had to leave school to earn some money. Her childhood was spent in the basement of what could only be described as a slum, a council flat in Stoke Newington, living hand to mouth with her brother, parents and a family of mice. Her childhood was Second World War London – rationing, bomb attacks, nights spent in the underground, evacuation, a joyous return, and then more poverty and hard work than any child should have to endure. But nothing could stop my mum. The only thing she would tell me was that money comes and goes, so make sure you have the character to face the world. She told me that I should mix with princes and paupers, and treat them both the same. A lesson I carried with me all the way to Buckingham Palace.

She met my dad, who'd left school to build and sell rabbit hutches, then caravans, during the Six-Day War in 1967. He stumbled upon her at the reception of a London hotel they were both staying in, as she was loudly berating the manager who had just refused to let two gay men check in. He instantly decided that this woman was for him. They soon moved in together, she started selling caravans too, and they settled into their pattern of seven-day work weeks, no rest, no holidays, no respite. Both my parents loved to work. And so my genes were firmly entrepreneur and sales based, as they sold caravan after caravan, and moved from slums to flats to houses, from market stalls and small towns to running businesses and holidays in Monte Carlo, from council flats to houses with a swimming pool. They were social mobility personified.

And so I entered the mix of fun and hard work, where-upon my folks decided to pack it all in and move from Surrey to Guernsey. I can't even imagine what a culture shock it was for my poor mum who went from glamour, independence and full-time employment – to island life, surrounded by women who didn't work, many of whom disliked her confidence. And for my dad, who went from workaholic to full-time retiree, at the age of fifty-one. What seemed like an amazing opportunity to retire young and enjoy life quickly descended into a mundane existence, a man who was no longer king of his domain, and instead at the behest of a new life, a new baby, and a community without the dynamism he had once enjoyed. He was also a manic depressive. Back before anyone really knew what to call it. And so, my mum was stuck on a new island, with a new baby, no friends, no family, no job, and with a partner who spiralled between elation and depression.

My parents were delighted that I showed academic promise and supported me in every conceivable way – but my childhood was the *Daily Mail*, the *Express*, *Coronation Street* and Jackie Collins. It was a very different upbringing to that of so many of my colleagues in later life. I was tabloid to their broadsheet, panto to their opera, Jilly Cooper (what a legend) to their Jane Austen. I didn't live in a world in which intellect, status and worth were measured by your understanding of politics, or history, or whether you could *speak* Latin.

By the time I was doing my A-levels, it was clear that I was going to university. This was a huge deal for my parents who had never had that chance. We had no idea how to apply or what you do. We were oblivious to the rivalries between certain places, that you can't apply for this one if you apply for that one, or even the massive impact that me deciding that Oxford and Cambridge were 'too snooty' could have on my future success. And so, my mum and I packed up and decided to visit all the places I liked the look of. We had baked potatoes in Norwich, a tour of the sights in York, and a very persuasive coach trip from the airport in Edinburgh. I don't know how most people decide where to go, but I can confirm that sharing an airport bus full of rugby players from Edinburgh Uni was pretty much 99% of my motivation for choosing to go there. It was a good starter city for someone who had always lived in the relative calm of island life. The culture shock was less stark than it would have been if I'd gone to LSE (not that I knew that at the time).

Of course, university didn't turn out to be all I had imagined. I'd expected lots of clever kids, hungry for debate and full of intellectual curiosity, grateful for this amazing educational opportunity, and instead I felt like I had stumbled into a group of largely uninterested teenagers, who took it for granted, and who were much keener on getting drunk than they were on discussing divine command theory or second wave feminism. I didn't drink, and so I ended up making a group of friends mostly outside university, and whiling away my days in cinemas and my nights dancing in the local clubs, bottle of water stuffed down my knee-high boots. The hiking, sailing, skiing, flat shoes and dinner parties beloved by my peers passed me by.

My first foray into news and current affairs issues – and the realisation that I knew very little – came when I joined the debating society. I loved it. I was one of two women (the other became Scotland's youngest ever female QC) and we absolutely revelled in our uniqueness. The more people made snide remarks about my sex, my clothes, my appearance, my arguments, the more I thrived. Their disdain inspired me.

We'd be given a topic ten minutes before we had to face the other teams, and a real Russian roulette of topics it was for someone like me. I can still feel the trepidation as I'd wait to see what the topic was. I'd be all set if it was something fairly current and general – animal testing, the death penalty, abortion or the environment – but, if it was

something requiring specific political or historical knowledge, I was screwed. The cold dread of seeing 'Israel' or
'European Union' would send my heart racing. I remember a particularly awful one, in St Andrews, where 'This
House believes that the situation in Northern Ireland is
intractable' had me and my nascent QC pal stumped, as
our combined knowledge of the topic could have filled
the back of a postage stamp, and the local students laughed
as we made one error after another. To protect myself
from further derision, I began to learn just about enough
to evade issues, but my knowledge base was clearly about
1% of many of the people I was competing against. If
you'd told them that, a decade later, I'd be briefing Jeremy
Paxman on everything from Irish politics to economics,
they wouldn't have believed you.

Despite several years of university and debating, I had
absolutely no idea what I wanted to do. Many of my peers
seemed to have known since they were born. I was still
struggling. Luckily, one of the lads in my class helped me
out. He was a confident and rambunctious rugby player
called Kerry. And he was very clear what he wanted to do.
He'd decided he was going to do a law conversion course
– three years crammed into one – and become a barrister
because, in his own words, he 'wanted to be paid for argu-
ing'. This struck a chord. It sounded ideal. I enquired

further, and he told me how hard it was to get a place, how arduous the course would be, how few people succeeded and how elite the group who did were. This didn't deter me – I researched the courses, spent hours and hours on my application, and sent it off to the same place – City University – that Kerry had applied to. I'd never really considered it before – my only knowledge was from *Ally McBeal* and *Prime Suspect*, but it seemed like a good fit. A few weeks later the results came back. I was in! I couldn't believe it! Kerry? Sadly, he didn't make it.

To be honest, I'd never even met a lawyer before I became one, and, with the benefit of hindsight, perhaps that wasn't my best move. The first day at law school was unforgettable. They listed the nine subjects we'd be studying across the year – effectively a three-year degree in nine months – and I was pretty sure I didn't know what most of them were. Equity and trusts, land law, EU law, contract, jurisprudence, tort. . . the list sounded like something from a bygone era. I told myself that it was good that I was a blank slate, and that I would pick things up. In truth, this was the most thrilling time of my academic life. I was lost for months – literally and figuratively – in a sea of new concepts, case law and seminars, guided by amazing lecturers, all of whom seemed to have written *the* text-book on their respective subjects. I immersed myself in the experience, started reading cases as if they were tales by Jackie Collins, and started teaching my brain to take in this new way of thinking. The work was relentless, and many students dropped out. I don't blame them – res ipsa loquitor! Caveat emptor! Promissory estoppel! Bonkers terms filled my mind with so many new ideas, and an intellectual discipline that has never left me. It was an incredible opportunity for someone like me, and I grabbed it with both hands.

When the finals came, it was like legal Hunger Games. I saw formerly confident, academically gifted people crumble and fall away. Some left early, some left late. By the time the two weeks of finals came – a three-hour exam every two days – we were like the finalists in *SAS: Who Dares Wins*. More people went to pieces. By the last day, grown men were crying.

I'd worked out by now that my love of debating, combined with my obsession with human behaviour, meant that criminal law was the route for me. I imagined myself sitting in cells with (alleged) murderers, striding the hallways of courts seeking justice for my clients, and carrying off the horsehair wig with aplomb. Of course, the reality – likely a 5 a.m. start at Euston for a ten-minute hearing in Wolverhampton – was a little less glamorous, but I was yet to find that out. At Bar School, I was

surrounded by classmates who strutted around as if they'd
already made it. They all wore suits and smart outfits,
while I remained in leather trousers. They were tweed to
my leopard print, satchels to my Gucci knockoff.

The modules were a new set of unknowns – civil procedure, criminal procedure, advocacy and, most crucially,
negotiation. I loved that class within moments. Mum's
family were market traders – the gift of the gab was something I really understood. Granted, other members of my
family had been dealing in lamb shanks and rabbit
hutches, sprats and caravans, but the skill set was identi-
cal. Added to that, most of my legal peers were way too
traditional to really go for the kill in those classes. They all
conformed to what was expected – a methodical analysis
of the facts, and a rigorous following of the rules of the
game. They would take in the situation, look for the weak-
ness in the case, set up their argument and present it in a
linear fashion. Me? I didn't know about the rules, and I
was their worst nightmare. I'd frustrate them over and
over by finding some loophole, a side issue, a circuitous
route they hadn't thought of, a bombshell fact or some
legal pun for laughs. I was in my absolute element. That
love of negotiation put me at the top of my class – although
my tutors seemed confused as to whether I was brilliant
or just a pain in the arse – and I thrived on my newfound

capability. I finally felt like I would be good at this, like it was all coming together, that I could *actually* make it, despite my background and lack of contacts. I applied for the barrister version of a training contract – a pupillage – and hoped for the best.

The interviews were genuinely hilarious, a cross between an interrogation and a horrendous first date. Sometimes I shone – with interviewers who appreciated someone 'different' – and sometimes I crashed and burned – with those who didn't. A particularly bruising exchange was with an Alice-band clad barrister called Philippa who left before the interview finished. She had asked me if Myra Hindley should ever be released. I clearly misread the room, and replied that if she ever completed her sentence and was deemed suitable to be released, then I would have faith in the administration of the justice system. This was clearly not what Pippa wanted to hear. Her voice rose as she began to list the names of the five children whom Hindley and Brady had butchered. It was a masterclass in how to destroy someone's argument with emotion. I never forgot that.

As luck would have it, I was offered a pupillage (somewhere else), became a 'baby barrister' and worked towards 'getting on my feet' (the phrase they used to describe the first time you stand up, palms sweating, heart pounding, in court). I had never felt prouder. Or more terrified.

My terror was not misplaced. Being a pupil barrister was mostly a living hell.

I can't even explain how hard I found it. I spent my days in a frenzy of anxiety, feeling the burden of the task ahead of me; people's fates would be in my hands. I did not bear the burden lightly. I felt constantly out of my depth. I've no clue if the other trainees were also in full panic mode, but they mostly appeared to carry their new responsibilities very lightly. They all seemed to be breezing through, working hard, drinking hard, laughing loudly. My life consisted of work only, no alcohol and definitely no fun. As time progressed, working six-day weeks, for about £500 a month, I realised more and more that this was not going to be the career for me.

The only time I felt happy was in the cells with the clients, or when I found out I didn't have a brief – a case – that day. Clearly that was problematic. I wasn't bad at the job – the solicitors liked me, and gave me plenty of work, and the clients mostly liked me too – but I was unhappy after a few months, despondent within a year, and fighting insomnia, hair loss and crippling anxiety before eighteen months were up. Two years in, I conceded defeat. I walked out of Chambers, and called my boss, my 'pupil master'. I thanked him for all his support and then explained I was certain that this, sadly, wasn't the job for me but that I was hopeful that the world would still be my oyster, in another profession.

Contempt dripped from his lips. 'Do you really think so?'

I walked home to the comforts of my sofa, jobless, with no income, with a career I had fought hard for in tatters. But that night I slept soundly for the first time in years.

1

From Paxman to McAlpine

And so, I sat on my sofa.

After a couple of days veering between extreme relief and blind panic, I came up with a plan. I would ask friends with interesting jobs if I could come and see what they did. One was an academic, another ran a charity and, as luck would have it, one worked on a programme called *Law in Action* at Radio 4. My friends kindly agreed and, a few months later, I found myself on the way to the BBC for a couple of days of work experience, shadowing my pal. It was immediately clear that the stress levels (low) and fun levels (high) of the BBC were a far better fit for my life ambitions, and so I made the most of my two days, treating it like a forty-eight-hour job interview. Of course, it would more than likely not lead to anything, but no one else on the team was a qualified lawyer, and the assumption that I knew about all areas of 'the law' was a huge help. I started coming up with ideas for news features straight away and relished long chats about the constitution or the latest high-profile divorce making headlines, and what that meant for case law and future marriages. It felt like a great fit and I was lucky to be offered six weeks on the programme. I would stay for eighteen years.

In all that time, the BBC remained a mystery to me. It's a privilege to be a part of – its status and reach are truly meaningful. But it's also a behemoth, housing enormous teams, tier upon tier of faceless managers and millions of emails.

When you arrive, you quickly learn the operation is run by the Director-General (DG) and he (it's never been a woman) seems to take on a Wizard of Oz kind of role. You feel his presence and his power without ever meeting him. In all my years there I only met one of them, Tony Hall, following the Prince Andrew interview.

Beneath the DG is a vast array of executives and managers. I rarely saw or dealt with them. They would crop up to make announcements, or to address us when something went wrong. You'd see them and assume you were in trouble.

The next layer is the actual lifeblood of the BBC – the journalists, presenters, correspondents, producers, researchers, editors, production assistants, camerapeople, floor staff. It's amazing how many types of jobs and specialisms there are. You could find everything from an expert in macroeconomics, to a specialist in Yemeni politics, someone who did the make-up for *Strictly Come Dancing* next to a leading cartographer. Once you're inside the building, you feel the true breadth of expertise, and the sense of possibility.

My career switch wasn't without issues. And when it came to the particulars of making radio – recording content, editing, what audio sounded good and what didn't, how to write a script – I was useless. So, I started learning fast, getting myself familiar with what it meant to 'produce'. The term covers such a multitude of possibilities in the media world and, given the variety of BBC output, it could mean completely different things on different programmes. You could be making tea, doing research and photocopying, arranging and recording interviews, briefing presenters and, sometimes, going on air as a correspondent or reporting on your own. I loved how every day was new and challenging, but with no one's life or liberty on the line. One week I would learn about obscure minutiae of the House of Lords (it was

Radio 4, after all) and the next week I could be interviewing someone who had secured an ASBO against a sheep, setting some kind of legal precedent in the process. Days would veer from long conversations about the future of family law, to taking the presenter, Marcel Berlins, to legal Chambers for an interview that would be hacked down to a mere five minutes in a tiny edit 'suite' back at Radio 4 HQ.

After a couple of years, Radio 4 started a new programme, called *More or Less*, about data and numbers. I was on the first team and worked with the amazing Andrew Dilnot – the economist and former Director of the Institute for Fiscal Studies – a man whose patience was tested by my basic questions about quantitative and qualitative data and the difference between a recession and stagflation, but who never ever showed it. I became his sidekick and got to report on everything from cancer clusters and women's fertility to how to measure animal populations by counting deer droppings. One particularly brilliant day involved driving the roads of Sussex, looking for dead hedgehogs to gauge their population, and hearing about how badgers massacre their spiky prey by tearing them apart, straight down the middle, like ripping open a Christmas gift, and gorging on their innards.

All went well for a number of years. I got married and had a child. Life rumbled on. I took a year off and came back to my old job. Except, as with many women who return from maternity leave, my exact job wasn't available to me anymore. My boss felt that I couldn't do the role part time, and so I got shuffled off into this Kafkaesque universe that the BBC calls 'development' – which seems to be an endless roster of pointless conversations and meetings about projects you never actually get to work on. I wasn't happy, and I was desperate to change roles. But the demands of parenting and logistics of childcare left me in limbo for a few months.

After a while, I started looking for other opportunities at the BBC. I'd always wanted to work at *Newsnight* – because I loved Jeremy Paxman's interviewing style – but, having had no experience either in news or live TV, it seemed a bit of a tall order, so I asked to spend a day with the team, just to see how it all worked, and thus began my campaign in earnest.

Walking into the *Newsnight* office was intimidating – and it takes a lot to intimidate me. The atmosphere on a TV programme is unlike radio. It's like going from a library into a nightclub. Radio takes itself very seriously – long, hushed conversations about macroeconomics or the state of global affairs, over cups of jasmine tea, wearing cardigans. Projects may take a day, or a week, or even months, and everything is treated painstakingly, and with the kind of attention to detail that having time to think allows. Television, and particularly news, is an entirely different creature. There was an immediate feeling of jeopardy, of danger, of excitement. The stakes felt high straight away, with everyone fuelled by a combination of coffee and adrenaline (there certainly wasn't time to eat).

I spent most of my first *Newsnight* editorial meeting writing down random names and acronyms, to be googled later, trying to keep up. The other producers were all very experienced, used to making five-minute television reports, from scratch, at a moment's notice. I tried to decipher their secret language – SOT (sound on tape, basically a clip with words), OOV (out of vision, when it's just pictures, no presenter in sight), VT (videotape – meaning a film or item that has been pre-recorded) – and the dizzying speed of it all took my breath away. I was told I'd be producing a segment, despite having never worked in news or TV before. The EOD – editor of the day – told me that I would be working on setting up a disco (not a dance, sadly, but TV speak for a discussion) about the Irish economy. They broke down exactly what that meant – finding and persuading experts, speaking to them and writing a brief, sorting all the logistics of the studios they'd be in, booking the 'line' (TV speak for sorting the technology that actually enables the interview to happen) and, most terrifyingly, briefing the presenter in person about what they needed to know and what questions they needed to ask to get the guest to provide interesting content. Or, more importantly, the 'news line' – that thrilling moment when a guest says something of political importance or something controversial – that makes it worthy of being repeated somewhere else.

I had nine hours before I would brief Jeremy Paxman – the most brilliant broadcaster of his generation – on what he should or shouldn't ask on a topic I knew nothing about, in a discussion I had to conjure up from scratch, for a show I was new to.

Every phone call would end with begging the potential guest to be mauled on live television by Jeremy Paxman, or by having to tell them that they weren't right for that evening's show. Handling egos was tricky – and trying to persuade people to come on was even harder. Before I worked at *Newsnight* I had assumed that people would generally be keen to come on. Not so. But of course who, other than a politician who is duty bound to do so, or perhaps an author, flogging (ahem) their book, would willingly expose themselves to possible humiliation?

Persuading reluctant people to do things was my forte, and I knew it. And so I persisted, finally securing two interviewees. The relief was immense. But then there were all kinds of technical issues that I was new to – studios had to be found and booked. 'Lines' had to be sorted separately. Taxis for guests. Collating information for Jeremy's brief. Finding time to go to the loo. Everyone was in a frenzy of activity all day. The VT (film) producers desperately called people to do short interviews, dragging camera crews across London and the country, against seemingly impossible deadlines, while correspondents ran from edit suites to outside settings to capture ten minutes of answers that would end up being forty-five seconds of television. There was a whole team of people who worked on logistics – called 'assignments' – and another that worked solely on graphics – the maps or pictures of data that pepper *Newsnight* films. Everyone was working fast and hard.

Paxman arrived sometime in the afternoon, looking exactly as imposing and, frankly, grumpy as you'd expect, but his interactions with other team members seemed congenial and laughter filled his office. I was surprised at how much autonomy I was given – I was literally told to 'write a two-page brief with questions' for Jeremy. That was it. As my time to meet him drew closer, I felt the same way as I had before courtroom appearances in front of a judge – clear in the knowledge that I would be facing someone who knew a million times more than I did but pretending it didn't faze me. Showing mettle, while knowing that, at any second, a slip-up could cost you everything.

This was the moment I realised that my actual words and questions could be spoken by him later that night. I hadn't fully understood that before I worked in TV – how much the producers influence what presenters say and do. I had assumed that, a bit like barristers, presenters were walking encyclopaedias, experts galore, with every piece of data and information at their fingertips. Of course, someone like Jeremy often needed very little from us – he was as close to that encyclopaedia as anyone I have ever worked with – but, nonetheless, we were expected to provide those essential facts, and contradictory quotes, those moments that trip a guest up, that are beloved by *Newsnight* viewers.

The lot of a producer is a strange one. When everything goes right? More likely than not the presenter or corre-spondent will get the credit. But, when it goes wrong, you can be damn sure some poor producer is getting shouted at.

Somehow, I didn't get anything wrong that day. And while it'd be an exaggeration to say that Jeremy took a liking to me, he didn't dislike me and so I considered that a win. My segment passed without obvious error and I was hooked. I had to find a way to stay.

The next day, I threw myself on the mercy of the very lovely Editor at the time, Peter Barron, and begged him to give me a chance. He'd had good feedback on me and agreed to let me stay for another six weeks. If I proved myself, I could stay.

While I was at *Newsnight* a lot changed in my life. I went from being married to getting divorced, and learning to adapt to the logistics of single parenting. One minute I would be sitting in a sandpit, scraping poo from a nappy, and the next day I could be in Downing Street, recording an interview with a government minister. The contrast really suited me and motivated me even more to score big interviews and high-impact guests when I was on the 'desk' (newspeak for being on the team that puts together the daily programme).

One day I was editing an interview with the writer Christopher Hitchens after he had been waterboarded (yes, really . . .) and the next day I would be off to Westminster, prepping questions for Alistair Darling, Chancellor of the Exchequer. Perhaps the other producers were used to this kind of lifestyle and mixing in these kinds of circles, but for me it was uncharted territory. I accepted my own ignorance of a lot of the terms and content, and threw myself into learning quickly, especially to avoid embarrassing mistakes. While the other producers fought over who'd get to do the lead VT (the first film in the programme, usually considered the most high-profile job of the day), I would ask over and over to arrange the first discussion instead. I loved booking those guests more than anything. And so, accidentally, I became a 'booker'. Though I didn't even know the term at the time. It was only when a colleague called me a 'top booker' that I realised this was the role that I wanted. I'd found my passion.

Now and again, I had to make a film and, to be honest, they weren't great. I just didn't have the eye or the inclination. And I knew most people didn't remember them, however beautiful they were. If you asked people what *Newsnight* was about, they'd always mention Paxman's interrogations, like when Treasury Minister Chloe Smith effectively ended her career under Paxman's cross-examination, the time he called Russell Brand 'a very trivial man', or addressed Dizzee Rascal as 'Mr Rascal', or when the EU economic affairs spokesman stormed off the set mid-interview, or the time former Home Secretary Michael Howard was asked the same question twelve times (although, that great interview was actually due to a technical issue – Paxman was forced to stall, asking the same question again and again). But this was the stuff of television history and I wanted to be a part of it.

The Editor, Peter Barron, spotted my enthusiasm and agreed to give me a job.

Little by little, I developed a contact book that allowed me to find pretty much anyone of significance faster than any other producer on the team. Luckily, this was the time before Twitter really took off. Now, it's very common for some unsuspecting producer to find their text exchanges or desperate emails plastered all over Twitter when an irate guest gets dropped at the last minute. It's a minefield. Usually, producers are on relatively low salaries (sometimes less than 10% of what the presenters can earn) and are facing very high stakes. Angry guests mouthing off on Twitter about us was yet to come.

Of course, things sometimes went wrong. One time, I sent Jeremy to interview the disgraced media mogul Conrad Black. During the interview, Paxman referred to Lord Black's wife, journalist Barbara Amiel, as 'a very extravagant wife' to which Lord Black responded, 'Oh God, I am going to throw up.' About halfway through, Lord Black was so enraged that he called Jeremy a 'priggish, gullible British fool' and said he'd done well to get through the interview without smashing Jeremy's face in.

'Well, you go ahead,' Paxman retorted. 'Well, no, I don't believe in violence,' Black responded (phew!). Luckily, Jeremy thought it was hilarious and, of course, those lines uttered from Black's mouth were repeated and reprinted everywhere and they still exist, in perpetuity, in part because I persuaded him to come on that day. It could have gone worse – later that day Black called Adam Boulton, from Sky News, 'a jackass'. Better a fool than a jackass in my books.

Another day, we had an interview with Mark Thompson, Director-General of the BBC at the time. It wasn't in the best of circumstances, as he was coming on to explain the mess caused by Russell Brand, who had prank-called the *Fawlty Towers* actor Andrew Sachs. The prank call became known as 'Sachsgate' – after Brand and Jonathan Ross left several, um, 'hilarious' messages on the actor's answerphone, including one in which Brand said he'd had sex with Sachs's granddaughter, Georgina Baillie. Mr Sachs was furious, and Mark Thompson was in the firing line. As for myself, working on a piece and interview with the man who runs the Corporation was not exactly my idea of fun. As luck would have it, the producer I was working with, Clare Walmsley, spotted that evening's stellar content on BBC 4 – a large number of reruns of a fascinating programme called *Skippy the Bush Kangaroo*. As the

Director-General tried to state that the BBC was a very serious and respected organisation, with a broad mix of content, Paxman grabbed the schedule Clare had given him, and dead-panned, in a very slow voice, the delights airing on BBC 4 that very evening. The DG's face was like thunder. We were all in hysterics. The atmosphere in the Green Room after the programme was a little frosty, to say the least.

The *Newsnight* Green Room was typically idiosyncratic – we had a small room for guests to wait in before and have a drink in after (tepid wine, often from a box, or a Diet Coke). Away from the office desk, you could go in, meet and greet your guests, and then bump into virtually anyone. In those tiny rooms, I rubbed shoulders with Earl Spencer and Martin Bashir (more on him later ...), Simon Schama (introduced me to martinis), Tony Benn (lovely and gave me advice on parenting), Harriet Harman (friendly and funny) and David Cameron (so much taller than I expected!). The realms of politics and journalism would temporarily coalesce – and, as it happened, many *Newsnight* staff would go on to work in politics: Sir Robbie Gibb as Theresa May's Director of Communications; Thea Rogers as George Osborne's Chief of Staff (and subsequently his fiancée). We shared gossip and jokes that would never leave those four walls, but friendships (and valuable connections) endured well beyond the room.

Once, Ann Widdecombe told Jeremy in the Green Room late one night that she would be appearing on *Strictly Come Dancing*. To illustrate her intent, she blithely lifted her tight-clad leg high into the air and plonked her foot on the top of the sofa, just a few inches away from Jeremy's face. I can still see his slow-motion expression of pure shock. I think it's the only time I ever saw it.

And so the years passed happily. My son, Lucas, was thriving, and so was I. I loved my job with a passion and we were, cliché of clichés, a real family at work.

But then, in 2013, in spectacular and public fashion, it all came crashing down.

The Jimmy Savile scandal broke. *Newsnight* had allegedly cancelled the transmission of an investigation into accusations that Savile had been a prolific sex offender. Careers were ended, inquiries were launched, *Panorama* investigated us, the country looked on, appalled, demanding an explanation for the BBC's safeguarding failures. I wasn't involved in the production or reporting of that story in any way, I wasn't in any of the many editorial meetings, increasingly fraught, with the (sadly deceased) reporter Liz MacKean and the brilliant, fiery senior producer Meirion Jones – as they clearly fought with the

Editor Peter Rippon. A black cloud descended on the office. Voices were raised, doors were slammed, people looked more and more anxious. Instead of reporting the news, we were the news. The Editor was being pursued by photographers, the front of the building was peppered with TV crews from other organisations, the office was full of various BBC executives, who we never usually saw, having hushed conversations with our, by now, ashen-faced Editor. Inevitably, heads rolled. By the end of that dark period Peter Rippon had been moved aside and Meirion Jones would later leave the programme.

It felt like a miracle *Newsnight* wasn't axed.

And then things got even worse.

As the review into the Savile investigation began, a new scandal was about to drop. A journalist called Angus Stickler, who worked for the Bureau of Investigative Journalism, brought the programme a story. It was about the alleged cover-up of a paedophile ring. And the story was about the possible involvement of a former Conservative Party Treasurer, Lord McAlpine.

The intention wasn't to name him but a series of unfortunate events, misunderstandings and tweets linked him by name. It was a total shit show. After dropping the Savile story, if we'd avoided a story about a Lord being an alleged paedophile, it could be a fiasco. But there was one thing far worse – to falsely and incorrectly accuse someone of being a paedophile when he wasn't.

The Director-General, George Entwhistle, resigned. More careers ended. I was certain we could not survive this new, terrible blow. It really felt like the end.

But, yet again, there was another change of leadership. The temporary Editor, Liz Gibbons, who had stepped in when Peter Rippon left, was gone, and various new faces arrived. Each time, we'd have to acclimatise to a new boss, try and impress him or her, when, in truth, most of us wanted to go home, close the door, cry and never come out ever again.

A few months later, it was announced that we'd be joined by the former Deputy Editor of the *Guardian*, Ian Katz. He would be something like my sixth Editor in two years. And so, here I was, back to trying to make my mark on a new boss, all of us rebuilding a brand that had fallen into disrepute.

2

Unknowable Fathers:
Brigitte Höss

The email arrived at 22.40 on Sunday 8 September 2013. Subject: 'Now here's a challenge . . .' I knew I shouldn't look. I knew looking would mean not sleeping, but I couldn't resist. After all, it was from the new Editor, Ian Katz, and we were all trying desperately to impress him. He'd just arrived from the *Guardian* and his reputation for clearing out staff and installing new people had preceded him. When it comes to news programmes, you're only as good as your last 'get'. Throw in a new Editor who is clueless about your track record and your anxiety reaches new heights.

I had good reason to be anxious too given the smell of restructuring in the air. And I wasn't entirely sure that he'd taken to me. So, this email felt crucial to my survival. Unfortunately, around this time my father had become extremely unwell. Though he would never articulate it as such, it became apparent that he was terminally ill. He was losing weight rapidly, with diminished energy and enthusiasm on the phone. I suppose that, living in different parts of the world, and rarely meeting up, he didn't want to burden me. And so, we kept our merry pretence going – him saying that he was feeling fine, me saying that all was going well at work. Neither sentiment was true.

By now I was secure in what I did and in my place on *Newsnight*. I hadn't made any major mistakes and felt like I was useful to the programme. But I wasn't confident I could ride out the structural changes. My gut told me that the only way to make it would be to put myself beyond reproach – to make myself invaluable all over again. It was exhausting. But, when you're a single income household, there's not much room for movement. Sure, there were other places I could work, but I loved the job and really wanted to stay. So, each challenge, each task, each request came steeped in the expectation that if I failed, I would be in an ever more perilous position.

So, a few seconds past 22.40, I opened the email.

It was addressed to four of us, so speed was everything. I scanned the contents – Ian had sent a link to an article in the *Independent* entitled 'Heaven in Auschwitz: Living as a killer's daughter'. The daughter in question was Brigitte Höss, child of Rudolf Höss, the Kommandant of Auschwitz. It was Rudolf Höss who designed and built Auschwitz. His was the brain behind Hitler's infamous concentration camp. By the end of the war, over a million Jews, and others, had been killed there. As such, Brigitte's father was one of the foremost mass murderers in history.

Between the ages of seven and eleven, Brigitte lived with her parents and four siblings in a villa next door to Auschwitz. She went on boat rides with her father, had picnics with her mother, and played in the sand while prisoners in striped pyjamas walked behind. It was, so she said, a normal childhood, spent alongside an arena of misery, torture and murder.

As I scanned the article, something else jumped out at me – although she had spoken to the writer, Thomas Harding, for this article, she had never spoken on record until that day. She hadn't told some of her later-life family about her past. She had never given a radio or TV inter-view. She had deliberately lived in the shadows, avoiding all public scrutiny. For decades she lived anonymously in a small house on a quiet street in North Virginia. For decades she stayed silent, safe from recrimination. And now, my new boss wanted us to find her and persuade her to appear on a global news network. Even I was taken aback. Perhaps it was an April Fool's trick. But it was September.

The next morning, I rushed into the office, and asked for more details on what Ian was thinking. My way to try to mark this as my project. He handed me a scrap of the article I had feverishly read the night before. 'Do you really think you can do this?' he asked – with a hint of incredulity. I wasn't sure I could, it already seemed impossible, but I knew I had to try. And so, I replied, 'If I can't, no one can.' And then hoped he hadn't seen that I was blagging. 'OK then, you can try first.' Challenge accepted.

Unbeknownst to him, I had a small head start. The author of the article on Höss, and its accompanying book, was someone I knew about. Thomas Harding had written the book because of his personal stake in the tale – Hanns Alexander, his great-uncle, was the man who eventually captured Höss. I'd been pitched various previous things he had written, and so knew his publisher. I was hoping I could persuade him to ask Brigitte to be interviewed on my behalf. I just wasn't sure what on earth would possess her to agree, but that would be my next challenge. Finding the 'sweet spot' that motivates someone is tricky. Usually, the upside is obvious – publicity, self-promotion, a wish for vindication, a desire to have your story told – but this time, none of those seemed likely to persuade her. She had no book to sell, no film to promote, no political party to defend. Nothing but a life in the shadows as the child of one of the most brutal killers in recent history.

I scrambled to get in touch with my contact, explaining our ambitious plan to interview this previously invisible woman. As we communicated, I started to try to put myself in her position: what was it that had finally motivated her to speak to Thomas – personal connection, a wish to talk about her father before it was too late, a need to assuage some associative guilt? What is the thing that would motivate a recluse to put herself on the line and actually agree to an interview with a programme she's probably never even heard of?

One thing could prove handy: Thomas had a book to sell. His motivation to promote his content for the huge global BBC audience could also be a powerful incentive for him to try to persuade her to participate.

Being honest, I didn't think there was a chance in hell that she would agree. But, I spoke to Thomas at length about the plan. About how we would try to get her to take this one chance to put her story on record for posterity, for the world to see. We both realised that her fears for her own safety, on that leafy quiet street in North Virginia, would be a major impediment. Not only would she be exposing herself to possible recrimination, but any local family members may also be identified, shocked, put at risk, intimidated, hunted down. So, we agreed the interview would have to be anonymous, with her face and voice distorted, so that she wouldn't face that danger.

Anonymous interviews are not without complication. First, you have to get editorial permission to offer it – and the reasons are strict. Fear for personal safety is one of them, but that's offset by the need for the audience to see the 'truth', look the person in the eye, hear their real voice. Usually, this kind of treatment would be for victims of sexual abuse, children, or people on the run from cartels or terrorist groups. 'My father was a mass murderer' was atypical. Luckily, my immediate boss saw the issues straight away. And realised that the public service element – to hear direct from Brigitte's mouth about her experience, her father, her time living at Auschwitz, her possible regrets – would be a powerful reminder of the evil that Rudolf Höss had committed and, for us, a once in a lifetime interview opportunity.

The next challenge was to strategise with Thomas about how to persuade her, what we could offer, how we could conduct the interview. It was hard to concede that, this time, I wouldn't be able to do the negotiation alone, or even have the chance to speak with her face to face. I had never been in this position before. I was going to have to trust someone else to take my ideas, my words, my pitch, and deliver it all in my absence, without any control. But it was Thomas's connection, his hard work that had tracked her down, he who had persuaded her to talk once already. I had to trust that he was absolutely the only person who would have the best chance again.

If Brigitte agreed, the logistics were daunting. I could barely take them in. Thomas was in the States, so could get to her if necessary, but we had no supporting infrastructure. And no one from the team nearby. We were so far away from making it happen that I tried to push the possible problems to the back of my mind. I would deal with them if, by some crazy miracle, she said yes. Thomas took all of my suggestions on board and we bounced ideas back and forth, tried to cover every possible eventuality. I know that he too thought that this was an impossible dream – it had taken him so long to negotiate his own interview, and that was 100% safe for her to do. This, however, would expose her to a whole new range of possible dangers that she had deliberately avoided for almost seventy years. People could start harassing her about her father, there could be threats, violence, attacks. I couldn't imagine her saying yes.

And then, she did.

Thomas said she felt she wanted something on record, despite her misgivings. And she knew her age meant the opportunity might not arise again. So, we had to make it happen. Here were just a few of the problems. One: she had only agreed on the basis that Thomas would interview her, a nightmare for our editorial control, and a huge responsibility for him. Two: we had no producers in that part of the world, and she wanted to do the interview 'right away'. Three: we needed a cameraperson, pronto. Four: I worked part time, it was the end of the week, I was meant to be looking after my six-year-old all weekend, and I had no experience whatsoever of arranging this kind of operation. I was out of my depth.

By now it was Friday night, and it looked like she wanted to do it on Monday. I had no choice but to contact Ian and his deputies, Rachel Jupp and Neil Breakwell. There was a fine line between looking incompetent and just being inexperienced, but I knew my own shortcomings, and we had the interview – that was the hard part – so I hoped we could find a way between us to make it happen.

Emails went back and forth in a frenzy. Six-year-olds aren't interested in interviews or logistics and so, as I took the emails and calls, tried to find a crew, tried to speak with Thomas about content, tried to get the Washington DC office to kindly help us, I had promised a trip to the cinema. I took one call while buying popcorn and drinks in Pret (to smuggle in . . .), I took another on the 220 bus to Westfield, faked the need for the loo to take the next call in a cubicle while my boy was next door, wrote one last email as the lights went down before some film started involving animated animals (they all morph into one). As any working single parent knows, you don't have much of a choice. You can't leave your child with someone else. So, I was that person with their little blue screen interfering with the big screen. We had stage one in place – a brilliant local cameraman called Pete Murtaugh could get to Thomas in time. Rachel and I were coming up with questions over email, and we had enough questions planned to make a fascinating interview. I dared to believe we could make it work. But as a cat and pigeon were fighting on the screen before me, I received a message from Thomas.

'Hi Sam. I am heading down to DC . . .'

I scanned the email and gasped. The interview was meant to be in two days. But now Thomas was saying he had a camera of his own, and was going to attempt to film it himself. And that he was going to do it in three hours' time.

I couldn't believe it. Everything that had been falling into place came crashing down. I called Rachel (my son was running on bribes of a toy and an ice cream) and we agreed to still try to get the cameraman to Thomas. At the very least, Pete could ensure the interview looked great, that the lighting was right, that the audio was correct. Setting up the correct ingredients for a TV interview is a tortuous affair. Many camerapeople are artists in their own right. Each one has particular quirks about how they like everything to look, certain rituals and methods to check the lighting, the sound, the camera angle, the position of the interviewee. All the mics have to be checked and tested. As a producer, when you're on site at the set up you'd take the role of one of the people in the chair, make sure the angles and heights were right, give a few words for the sound levels, hold a piece of white paper in front of your face for the white balance, check that you've turned off any noisy air conditioning, or moved any noisy people out of the room. I usually allow ninety minutes for the whole process, to make sure it can be done thoroughly and without the crew feeling like they are being rushed. It was clear that would be impossible here, given how jumpy Brigitte would be, but at least Pete would be able to get it looking broadcast ready. And Thomas had all of our questions and was obviously an adept interviewer. Perhaps everything would be OK after all?

Lucas was distinctly unimpressed by my behaviour, but I had no other choice. I took the path of least resistance, and offered not only an ice cream, but a topping. He eyed me very suspiciously. I am not a parent who uses bribery for good behaviour. Ever. He sensed this might be some kind of trap, so kept questioning if he could 'realllllly' have a topping? YES! Just this once. His eyes lit up, and he opted for hundreds and thousands.

Just as he took his first, thrilled, lick, the phone buzzed again. What now?

The new complication was a potential final straw. Brigitte would not let Pete into her home. It was Thomas alone. Or nothing.

We spoke to Pete – he was very calm in the circumstances. I was not. He had arranged to meet Thomas, who was in a separate car heading to Brigitte, in a layby. He felt sure he could teach him enough in twenty minutes to get Thomas filming, on his own personal hi-tech camera, to a standard that would be broadcastable. I wasn't so sure. An impossible interview, in impossible circumstances already, and now we might get something that wasn't of a high enough quality to use. All of Thomas's hard work, all of my hard work, could end up on the cutting room floor. And it wasn't like we could go back for a reshoot. To make matters worse, she had asked for no communications once he was on site, and we wouldn't be able to see the material for hours. Maybe not even until the next day. I couldn't bear it. Lucas finished his ice cream, we purchased a toy and made our way back to the house. He was chatting away, nicely distracting me from the stresses of my career.

The hours waiting for Thomas to emerge from the interview were torturous. I sat on the sofa pathologically checking my phone. Nothing for an hour. Then two. Each minute felt longer than the last. I knew that, despite all the hard work, if we ended up with something shoddy, we might as well not have bothered.

And so, I waited, and waited, desperate for some news.

Lucas was playing with some sand. It felt inconceivable to me that, at around the same age, our interviewee had lived alongside a genocidal mastermind. Her father was, in the worst possible way, extremely skilful – by 1944 up to two thousand people were being killed in the camp each hour. After his arrest he was taken to Nuremberg and put on trial. Rather fittingly, after he was found guilty, in April 1947, he met his end hanged on a gallows next to the old Auschwitz crematorium. From that point, the Höss family reinvented themselves. And in the 1970s Brigitte had moved to the suburbs of Washington DC with her husband. And what of that terrible past? She had told her husband. She hadn't told her children. Or her friends. But she was about to tell us.

Finally, the phone pinged again. The interview was over. She had answered all of our questions. Pete had taken a look at it and thought it would be 'fine'. That word filled me with cold dread. It sounded like a euphemism – cameraman speak for 'not good at all'. But I had no choice but to wait until Monday, when I would be able to see the transferred files in the flesh, able to gauge whether what we had would make the grade.

One of the peculiarities of my job is that I rarely edit the interviews myself. Because I am trying to generate the content, trying to make so many interviews happen, that takes up all of my time, and so once the interview has been recorded, someone else on the team makes the final decisions about what makes it to air and what gets left behind. In truth, I'm also not very good at the 'pictures' part – I don't possess the artist's flair for visual beauty, that obsessive desire to make every frame unforgettable. My passion is for making the content unforgettable, for seeing it travel far beyond the programme, onto the website, into the papers, onto other parts of the network, existing in digital perpetuity.

On the Monday, the producer took us into the edit suite. As I had suspected, although Thomas had done a brilliant job in the circumstances, the quality was touch and go. But, we all sat down to watch what Brigitte Höss had to say for the first time in her life. The room fell completely silent.

To protect her identity, we had to cover her face in the final broadcast, 'blobbing' as we call it, and change the tone of her voice. But, in that room, we all watched her as she sat before Thomas, in full view, with her own voice, answering his questions as the person she really was.

The woman before us sat on the far right of an old white sofa, adorned with one black cushion and one floral one. The wall behind her was covered in dark wood panelling, with what looked like a dreaded air conditioner dominating the room. She wore a simple black dress, arms bare, reading glasses hanging around her neck, a black bangle and a black watch. Semi-slumped against the side rest of the chair, she used her hands frequently and expressively. I couldn't imagine how she felt talking about this on camera, for the first time, knowing that any part of this conversation could be seen in homes, bars and airports across the world. By families who may have lost relatives because of her father. In countries whose Jewish populations had been decimated by his acts. Her next-door neighbour could be watching. Perhaps one of them had had tea with her earlier that day. Perhaps someone would recognise the ornate cushion. Maybe her children didn't know she was doing this. Would they too recognise that room, that watch, finally find out who their relatives had been?

Thomas asked his first question. What was her childhood in that deadly home like? The room held its breath. She replied slowly, in English with a Germanic accent, tilting her head to the camera. 'I loved it, it was like paradise for me, and I didn't know what was on the other side of the villa.' Our headline, immediately.

It was an unnerving experience. She spoke of an idyllic childhood with a nostalgia I could relate to and with a man she described as 'the nicest man in the world'. My stomach lurched. I was not without my own connection to this story. My grandfather had been raised in Poland, he was Jewish, and some of his relatives had fled before Hitler took his lethal toll. Some of them. My grandfather was one of the lucky ones, and never spoke of what he may or may not have experienced, and those relatives who had faced a different fate. Growing up, I had always felt the shadow of what happened on my shoulder – I was only a quarter Jewish, and an atheist, but that would have been enough to consign me to the fate that Höss meted out. My grandfather never went back to Poland – he had always been scared to return there, even decades later. He wouldn't even venture into France. Certainly not to Germany. It was only in his adopted country that he felt safe. He started work as a tailor, he changed his name, left his past behind, pretended it had never happened, created a new family – my mother, Brunetta (she hates the name), and a son, Maurice, who met an early death in a motorcycle accident. My grandfather never spoke of him either.

As my grandmother wasn't Jewish, and it passes down the maternal line, my mother had been raised in an unfortunate limbo – Jewish enough to be teased and ridiculed by some of her peers, and not Jewish enough to be accepted by the community around her. Her experiences in childhood limbo made her a resolute atheist for her entire life.

My attention flipped back to the interview as Thomas pressed Brigitte more – how was it credible, he asked, especially as the prisoners had helped around the house, in the garden, no doubt decked in their grim pyjamas, that she hadn't realised something was wrong? Seen some horrific act that alerted her to some aspect of her father's enterprise?

'We didn't know what else was there,' she insisted. 'My father never talked about things like this, and there was no smoke, there was no smell of something. He said, "Oh, my darling, did you have a nice day?" and then he hugged us all. But it seems sometimes he was not very happy, I mean he was nice, but I could see things maybe bothered him also. But, because I am sure, he wanted to get away, but if you're in something, you are in.'

Thomas went on, 'You said he was the nicest man in the world? How is that possible?' In reply, her voice slowed; she knew her answer would sound extraordinary to the world, given what we now knew he had been doing. 'Yes, I don't know. There was not one flaw in him, nothing that was mean or not nice. At first I didn't believe it, I said couldn't be him. But now I believe, but I don't believe he did it himself. Definitely not. Himmler and Hitler . . . pushed . . . I don't think it was his idea, I could not believe a man who was so warm at home could do something like this. I believe bad things happened there. He managed it, but I think he didn't start it.'

He was 'just' the manager. That was how she rationalised this to herself. A life spent in denial of a father who was a mass murderer. An inability to accept that he was responsible for that horror. Finally, she conceded that he had done something, but in the way only a daughter, who loved someone dearly who turned out to be evil personified, could do. 'So there were two sides to your father, you think?' Thomas asked. 'Definitely . . . he couldn't be a person so gentle and wonderful and so family orientated and he can do something like this? I just know the good side, I don't know the bad side, and I think I am glad about it.'

The interview was remarkable. One of those rare occasions where you feel you have been given access to something singular. Literally something that no one has ever seen before. We all had chills and Rachel deemed it broadcastable. I was extremely relieved.

As I left the edit suite, I called my own father. He had his own connection to this tale. He was a young man when the Second World War began, and had been called up to join the army. He had served for several years, mostly in France, somehow evading the dreadful fate that befell so many of his friends. He never spoke of it either. He only told me one tale about his time there during my entire life – he'd been a very talented cricket player, even spotted once by the famous Australian cricketer Don Bradman, who took the time to write to the boy who worshipped him, sending him a letter saying how great he was. The letter still took pride of place in his office, decades later. My father was never able to cull his competitive nature, even against me as a child. I recall playing cricket with him as a little girl, consistently unable to ever hit the ball, while, however appalling my throw was, my father would somehow lob the ball over the house. It was three storeys. And he did it every time. We would laugh so hard that my mum would come out to see what was happening. He just couldn't resist showing off his batting prowess. This particular skill had saved his skin one day while serving in France – he was meant to go to the front, but an impromptu squad cricket game began, and my father, as the star player, had been asked to stay behind to play. It may have saved his life. Some of his closest friends lost their lives that day, blown to bits. He only mentioned this once.

In a much less acute way, we were complicit in our own denial. As ever, I asked routine questions about his lunch, what he had watched on TV, how his football team was doing, what was happening with the garden, whether he had seen any bunnies or sheep. And he reciprocated with his own rote, asking about Lucas, whether he was doing well at school, if he liked cricket, what I made of the latest political shenanigans (we never agreed). He would ask how the new boss was doing, as he now knew I had been having some issues, about whomever I was dating at the time, what I was having for dinner (takeaway at my desk, no doubt). We both studiously avoided the elephant in the room. His own mortality.

At least when I called the next time, I had some good news. Ian had emailed me after the interview aired. 'Just

wanted to say big well done on making Höss happen.
Great get.' It felt like the beginning of a reprieve. Although
many people around me were leaving, or being sacked, I
remained hopeful that this kind of achievement could
help me survive. My dad was delighted. I left him to his
football, he left me to my takeaway.

He died eight weeks later.

3

Moral Duty: Paul Flowers

'Sex, drugs, blasphemy, depravity, arrogance.' The *Mail on Sunday* headline on 23 November 2013 had it all.

A fall from grace. A high-profile man on his knees. Humiliation and titillation. Reverend Paul Flowers, the chairman of the Co-operative Bank, was a tabloid's dream. The Methodist minister, nicknamed 'The Crystal Methodist', had overseen the near collapse of the Co-operative Bank, which lost £700 million in the first half of 2013, and then was found to have a £1.5 billion hole in its finances, and this was only the start. Later that year, he was accused of buying and using crystal meth, crack cocaine and ketamine. There was the added lasciviousness to his sorry tale – accusations of a secret gay life, a supposed appearance on the dating app Grindr and an ill-advised friendship with a male escort. The tales of his demise dominated the headlines day after day.

Though *Newsnight* prides itself on intelligent, incisive journalism, a story like this, involving a failing bank, a disastrous select committee appearance and possible civil and criminal proceedings, would be high profile enough to make the cut. At the centre of it all was Reverend Flowers – a rotund, bearded, jolly-looking minister. A position he'd held for forty years. An interview with him would be a blockbuster and I was determined to track him down.

On programmes like ours, we like to think that we do something removed from day-to-day tabloid journalism. For some, there will be a certain snobbery about that world. There's a perception that the hard graft that fills those pages – door knocking, 'ambulance chasing', seeking out families of murdered teens or relatives of rape victims – is far removed from the upper echelons of the BBC. But that's not true. It's just a different group of people that we are chasing. And we want to collect headlines. We want to entertain.

For the Reverend, the revelations were a car crash. And like all car crashes, it's hard to look away. I knew that some of my work was tabloids on the TV. I was entirely comfortable with that. For me, it was all about humanity.

Inhumanity. We want 'sex, drugs, blasphemy, depravity, arrogance'. The space between my penchant for these sorts of stories and what *Newsnight* would more typically do meant I was that much more committed when I had the chance to indulge in the less intellectual side.

One of the reasons for going off the rails that Flowers would offer retrospectively was the death of his mother. This was easy to understand. I was a bit off kilter too. I'd assuaged my grief with tears and tequila, and I remained a mess. Two days before my father died, Ian, the new Editor, had called me into an office for one of his ominous 'chats'. My father was literally on his death bed, so the details are a bit hazy, but he'd told me that I wasn't 'on vision'. The conversation left me unsettled. I'd tried to fight back a little with examples of my many achievements, but I wasn't convinced that he cared. My father's subsequent death had taken me out of the office for a couple of weeks so that, when I returned, I felt the dual burden of grief and fear of what awaited me at work. At that time, the office inspired dread in many of us. People had started to leave – some voluntarily, some not – culminating in one of the presenters – Gavin Esler – discovering the end of his own time at *Newsnight* in a *Guardian* column. Several producers had been told that work placements were coming to an end, a couple of reporters were made redundant, their posts closed, and I honestly felt it was only a matter of time for me.

It had also been a tumultuous time for the star of the show – Jeremy Paxman. I certainly sensed a rift between the two men at the helm – a power struggle was brewing. Ian had seemed to fire a shot at Jeremy in various comments he'd made about liking less confrontational interviews and preferring more of a conversation than an adversarial row. That was inconceivable to me. Jeremy *was* the art of the interview, he was the master, and he had been at the helm of it all for twenty-five years. But his position seemed suddenly fragile and that made me even more worried – if the new Editor was targeting Paxman, none of us stood a chance! The only way I could respond was by trying to make myself indispensable, all over again. A kind of exhausting professional Groundhog Day.

A few months had passed since the Höss interview, and I needed another hit. Flowers seemed like the perfect opportunity. I had made a few attempts to find him, on the quiet, but my usual routes hadn't worked out. I needed a new tactic.

Then, the whole issue became urgent.

Ian had promoted one of my less experienced colleagues – a lovely, enthusiastic woman called Hannah – over me, and I'd never felt more vulnerable. She and I were now locked in a competition neither of us wanted to be in, she to prove herself in a role many had assumed would be mine, and I to try and save my neck.

Getting Paul Flowers became my lifeline. And Hannah had opened the contest explicitly with a jocular email titled 'FIRST ONE TO FIND PAUL FLOWERS competition'. The prize was a bottle of champagne, but we both knew the real prize was something far more important: job security. At least for a little while.

I'd never been an investigative journalist but finding someone who doesn't want to be found provided a little taster. I'd always start looking for the easy route – reading articles, trying to find a simple way to contact someone – a workplace, a lawyer, a PR representative, an agent. Next, it'd be a trawl of social media – did they have Twitter? Facebook? LinkedIn? Paul Flowers had none of these. Then you'd try the more complex routes – checking with Companies House if they were registered as a director for any businesses or scouring the online phone book for every P. Flowers there was. Followed by a number of awkward calls to complete strangers, going about their business, perplexed by your enquiry. I drew blank after blank. Then you'd try the electoral roll – and search for people there, even, in rare cases, send them a letter. Again, nothing came up. In desperation, I tried his old employer, the Co-operative Bank, but, quite understandably, they were either unwilling or unable to help.

In what felt like a final and pointless move, I googled Paul Flowers again. I trawled through every article I could find that mentioned him, hoping there would be some former colleague, previous employer, or a route I hadn't thought of. It's much easier to find someone whose star is on the rise – people are happy to pass on their details. But when things go pear shaped, everyone is decidedly more cagey. I found out that Reverend Flowers had been associated with particular Methodist churches, and I began to find their numbers and call their receptions. You can imagine the response. No one was ever rude, quite the opposite, but the firmness with which people were refusing to help me made it clear that I was going to need a miracle.

I couldn't bear to give up, and so I kept on, trawling some legal sites. And then, a glimmer of hope. Someone had written a short item about his case. A single practitioner lawyer in the north of England called Andrew Hollis.

I feel an immediate commonality when talking to lawyers. Andrew was a criminal defence solicitor, so I knew something of his work. I hoped that once I established our common ground there would be a level of trust or understanding that another journalist might not get. So, I emailed him with my number, asking for an off the record chat (everyone assumes every call is recorded and somehow dangerous if you don't say that) and hoped for the best.

I didn't hear anything for days. Life carried on as usual. An old friend, Maajid Nawaz, still an LBC radio presenter at the time, invited me for a cheer up dinner, and I trudged through Soho to a Mexican restaurant we both liked, hoping for some more grief-numbing tequila. Suddenly, my phone rang. It was an unlisted number, which I wouldn't usually pick up, but this time I did. The voice at the other end wasn't one I knew. 'Hey, Sam, it's Andy Hollis.' For a second, the name didn't compute, and he seemed to sense that and so he added, 'I'm Paul Flowers' solicitor.' My heart stopped, and I screeched to a halt in the middle of the street. This was my chance. I'd had some time to think about what would possibly persuade Flowers to speak, and I assumed there would only be two reasons. One would be the usual thing – to set the record straight – but the other one would likely be more personal – he'd faced an absolute onslaught of articles in the *Daily Mail* and the *Mail on Sunday*. It had been unremitting. I wondered if this could be my 'in'. The BBC is one of the *Mail*'s more popular enemies, and *Newsnight*, specifically, had come under fire over the years. Some of it entirely justified, some less so. I felt this was my forte. And so I said to Andy, 'Tell Mr Flowers, if he really wants to f**k off the *Daily Mail*, doing a *Newsnight* interview is the ultimate revenge!' I waited to see the reaction, as it was a risky move, but Andy Hollis bellowed down the phone, told me he'd let Reverend Flowers know, and then he'd get back to me. The call ended, and I could barely believe my luck. I ran to meet Maajid and regaled him with the story of my latest quest. And hoped, maybe even prayed, for a yes.

In that moment there's always a tactical decision to make. Do you let your boss know, and thereby claim some credit for the fact that you're getting close to the interviewee? Or do you keep quiet, in case it all falls through and then you look a fool? I felt like my old bosses would have been really impressed that I'd got so far, but I wasn't sure that anything other than a closed deal was worth mentioning in the current climate.

I didn't have to wait long to make my decision. The very next day Andy Hollis called back. 'He's up for meeting to discuss doing this. Will you come to Manchester to hopefully confirm it and answer his questions in person?' I was beyond thrilled, I was so close, and now was the time to tell Ian, and my Deputy Editor, Neil Breakwell. I couldn't wait.

Back in the office, the decision was made that Neil would be the one to go for the final conversation. What can I say – obviously I wasn't pleased, but there was nothing I could do. In truth, it made some sense – Neil was more senior and could reassure the Reverend about the editorial issues he might be worried about; he could address the concerns that I would have had to call him about anyway. He didn't have a kid to get childcare for, plus he was easy on the eye. We weren't beyond recognising that this could have a positive impact on the conversation. And so, I was left behind, and Neil made his way to meet the Reverend to try to make the final arrangements, promising me that he'd do his best for me, and thrilled at the progress I had already made. I felt we were already about 90% there – and I just had to hope that all of my hard work wasn't squandered.

Finally Neil called. Reverend Flowers had agreed. We would get the exclusive.

It was going to be his first interview since his arrest over the drug allegations, and we knew it was dynamite. Even Paxman was excited, in his own way. Neil chose a producer, and the team started its frenzy of activity to do the research and select the questions that would make the interview a success. As Flowers had been charged, we had certain restrictions on what we could ask, so we took legal advice. We knew he couldn't answer certain things as a result, but we could still ask the questions about it all – the sex, the drugs, the demise of the Co-operative Bank and his life since it had all fallen apart.

Ian was delighted and Hannah, graciously, was just as thrilled for me. I knew the coverage this would garner could be a crucial part in the rest of my career. I just hoped Reverend Flowers would deliver.

As it happened, I needn't have worried. When Jeremy and Neil came back from the interview, at some secret location in a city up north, it was clear they thought it'd gone brilliantly. They both had that kind of elated energy that only a scoop can bring. In Neil's case this manifested as actual beaming enthusiasm, in Jeremy's case in laconic understatement. 'Good get, Sam,' he said. 'He actually gave us some good news lines.'

By now, it was March 2014; it'd taken months to sort – and I couldn't wait to watch. A standard interview would be on air for about five minutes, perhaps between seven and ten minutes for a world leader. But, because it was a total exclusive, we'd decided to run it longer. At a whopping eighteen minutes. It'd be most of the programme. And, by now, the rest of the BBC had heard we'd got the prize, and the phones started buzzing, asking us what Flowers had said, and what clips – short sections of the interview that other programmes can run before it all comes out – would be available.

I sat down to watch it, the battle of the Reverend and the presenter, assuming Jeremy would eat him alive. That was what I was hoping for at least. The room chosen for the interview was strangely prosaic. Often, we get no choice about the room an interview is filmed in, and so you have to make the best of it and try to make the camera frame look a bit more interesting. Clearly, the cameraperson, or Neil, had decided that the bendy lamp was a good addition to the backdrop, but I found it distracting. Flowers himself looked rather congenial – not at all the cowed shell of a man I had been expecting. His face was almost cheerful, white beard, smart glasses, new haircut – kind of like a corporate version of Santa. Jeremy, in contrast, didn't look at all jovial. His backdrop looked like a toilet door, with a strategically placed lily to the left of his head. He sat languidly in an awkward office chair. But his questions were razor sharp. Off he went: 'What's this last year been like?'

There was an awkward silence. And then Flowers began to laugh. Bearing in mind the seriousness of the allegations against him – being an incompetent chairman, with a possible drug charge and a possible penchant for male escorts – it seemed an unfortunate opening response. 'Um, interesting. I was the chair of the board of the bank until late May and officially resigned on June 5th, which was actually my birthday, and so it was a joy to sign off on the job on my birthday.' He was clearly nervous, in a garrulous mood, and trying to avoid the more difficult questions, and so he just carried on, barely breathing. 'And for me personally, there have been several months when it has been hellish. Because I knew that I particularly needed to find some professional support for the issues that I was facing, I actually booked myself into a very well-known hospital for four weeks, from the end of November, until Christmas Eve. And underwent what was called their addictions treatment programme, for the twenty-eight days that I was there.' He spoke clearly and comfortably, warming to his theme. 'I found that both cathartic and traumatic, but it actually helped me to look at, not so much the superficial issues of the addictions themselves, but the more deep-seated reasons why people resort to any sort of addiction. And for me that was, I think, life changing. And I continue to go there every week for therapy.'

Finally, he stopped. Blinked, breathed and relaxed again. So far, so predictable – he was offering us his excuse for his behaviour. He clearly felt his addictions were to blame. He wasn't as scared as I'd assumed. He didn't look like someone who had presided over the near collapse of a bank. He looked like someone who was out for lunch with a friend. Paxman continued, 'Can we go back then to the question of the chairmanship of the bank? What was it that made you think you were qualified to run a bank?'

Still Flowers looked unperturbed, almost scolding Jeremy for the question in the tone of his reply. 'I didn't, and it wasn't my job to make a judgement about whether I was qualified. Others made a judgement that I was the right and appropriate person to be the chair at that particular time. There was a panel, which interviewed four of us, who were candidates for the job. I was the unanimous choice of that panel. I was then the unanimous choice of the bank board. I was then the unanimous choice of the group board. And I then went again to the FSA [Financial Services Authority], for a further interview, to see whether they thought I was fit to be chair of that bank board.' His expression was impassive, possibly irritated by the question.

And then I realised that something was going on. Perhaps it was imperceptible to someone who hadn't watched hours and hours of Jeremy's interviews, but it was apparent to me. Jeremy wasn't that interested in mauling him. His usual style – ferocious and forensic – was absent. He was bored! And that was apparent to Flowers too. His body language was changing. Instead of sitting back in his seat, looking somewhat defensive, he made a jaunty jab at Jeremy. 'I was prepared for this by a very hellish mock interview, a bit like you at your worst really, if I might be so bold. And they took me to hell and back in terms of questions. But the FSA had a really wonderful conversation about philosophy and ethics and issues that were around, and their panel approved me. So, it's not for me to make a judgement about whether I was qualified – a range of other people at the time said I was.' He looked very pleased with his own, extensive, answer.

Flowers breathed heavily. Paxman smiled. The expectations of fireworks waned. It was hard to tell if Jeremy had just had a bad day, or wasn't fully briefed, or if he had other things on his mind. But this had the air of two old pals having a chat about something tricky. It was, to use the worst criticism of all for a *Newsnight* interview, 'soft'.

Flowers warmed to his theme of being blameless. 'I wasn't put in as a banker. I was put in as a co-operator. A representative of the Co-op group. And I had a particular job to do in terms of governance, that was my role.' His words went on and on. I waited for the next killer question ... about his role in the disastrous merger with

Britannia Building Society, which was one of the causes of his downfall, but Jeremy just let him pass the blame to others. First the accountancy firm KPMG, then 'some fancy merchant bankers, who were paid vast sums of money to do it'. Whoever it was, all of them said that this was a good deal. The FSA didn't pick up that there were these major problems and certainly nobody in the City told him that there were . . . And then he moved to the proposed merger with Lloyds – how had that gone wrong? This time Flowers moved the blame to the government, saying that he'd been under pressure to make it happen. 'What form did this pressure take?' Jeremy asked. 'Regular calls, regular checks to see whether or not we were progressing well, and I mean, two or three times a week, calls from the Junior Minister,' Flowers said. 'They wanted a deal, and they wanted us to do it. They might say no now, but I know that was what they wanted, and that was the pressure they were applying.' Not my fault, not my problem, not my responsibility. This was the theme of every answer.

We were already six minutes into the interview, and, for a moment, I wondered if there were going to be any effective accountability questions. When was Jeremy going to stick the knife in? He started to lean forward in his chair, and eyeballed his interviewee with that infamous Paxman stare and a raise of his eyebrow. 'You're painting yourself as an innocent abroad . . .'

'No,' Flowers replied, 'I'm not innocent. I take full responsibility for the decisions that we took. And indeed, I resigned because I believed it was right for the chair of the board to take responsibility. Albeit that all the decisions taken were not by me personally, but by the board as a whole.' He was determined to take virtually no blame.

Finally, Jeremy was having none of it. 'But resignation was an admission of inadequacy, wasn't it?' Flowers replied, 'No, I think it was an admission that things had gone wrong, and that, as the person who was in the chair, I should take responsibility for it.'

It was clear that this interview was unlikely to have that magical moment where Paxman would elicit a mea culpa, some falling on his sword, a tearful apology. In fact, thus far, Flowers hadn't apologised or shown any remorse at all. What about his disastrous appearance at the Treasury Select Committee when he'd got the bank's assets wrong by a margin of over £40 billion? 'Ill-prepared' and 'put off' by the 'aggression' of biased MPs apparently. What about the loss of trust in banking? He said that it used to be run by people of honour and integrity and decency, but not so much anymore. It was clear that the Reverend saw himself as a moral man too. This was the perfect moment for

Jeremy to raise the litany of issues in his personal life. The allegations of drug taking, the dubious decisions about his sexual conduct, the much-publicised 'friendship' with a male escort. I was curious how Paxman would deploy this information. I glanced at the clock on the edit. There were only six minutes left.

Of course, I was hoping for so much more. There was a certain disappointment in how he was 'performing'. I'd never feel comfort seeing someone who was a victim of crime or whose family member had been murdered in any kind of pain. But this man? Someone who had been powerful and successful and messed it all up? Someone who had been embroiled in hypocrisy? This was the kind of discomfort I did look for. Perhaps others don't like to admit it but we are often itching for it. We look to create intrigue, discomfort and a certain jeopardy in the interviews. It's what 'news' really is.

Then, it began. Flowers let slip that one or two former bank colleagues had been in touch with him though they had been warned against it, and Paxman finally went in. 'So you've been cast into the outer darkness almost?' Flowers finally looked uncomfortable, no doubt wary of his religion, and the charges of hypocrisy, starting to seep into the conversation. Waiting for the dirty deeds to be raised. He shifted in his chair, moved around some more, averted his gaze. All classic signs to a presenter, and a producer, that your interviewee is starting to get worried. He stuttered and stumbled over his words. 'Well, I, I believe, that even in Dante's inferno there is the possibility of you crawling out of the pit.' Jeremy warmed to his religious theme: 'You've fallen like Lucifer?' And, just as quickly as it had come, the discomfort evaporated. Both men laughed, and Flowers looked comfortable again. 'Ummm, and where do you find Lucifer in the Bible, Mr Paxman?' And then they both laughed some more.

I thought we'd now lost the momentum, but, at last, the juicy questions arrived. 'Then comes, of course, all the horrible stuff for you when you're outed for drugs and rent boys and all that stuff. Had you been doing drugs while you were chairman of the bank?' I knew Flowers wouldn't answer this, as criminal proceedings were ongoing, and he gave an answer exactly to that effect. Of course, he only wished he could respond (as if!) but legal restraints didn't allow . . .

For a man who was so superb as taking politicians apart, Paxman was squeamish when it came to talk of sex. You could sense the distaste in his eyes when such matters had to be discussed, and so he side-stepped mentioning the salacious details, instead asking, 'When you saw what the *Mail on Sunday* printed about you, what did you think?' Flowers evaded yet again. 'I find the *Mail on Sunday* and its pseudo-fascist far right tendencies, which make Vladimir Putin look like a bleeding-heart liberal, utterly abhorrent. And the reality is that a considerable amount of what the *Mail on Sunday* printed has been pure and utter fiction.'

At this stage I expected Jeremy to read out the allegations. To ask, which part was fiction? The sex? The drugs? The blasphemy? The depravity? To make him squirm. But instead he returned to an area he was more comfortable with – his religious theme. 'Given your religious background, do you think you have sinned?' Flowers finally looked somewhat contrite. His discomfort with the religious questions was writ large all over his face. He paused. Finally, surely, he was going to say he'd actually done something wrong. 'Forgive me, it's always much more complex than that. Of course I have. And I am in company with every other human being for having my frailties, and some of my fragility, exposed. Most people get through life without that ever coming into the public domain. I am no better and no worse, it seems to me, than any number of other people, ummm, but of course I have sinned in that old-fashioned term, which I would rarely use, I have to say. But, I'm like everybody else, I am frail.'

I know that would, finally, be our news line: 'Paul Flowers admits he has sinned.' That would be in every BBC bulletin, in every news headline, in every broadsheet and tabloid in the land. I felt palpable relief. An admission like that would run all over the country. We were at fifteen minutes. He'd finally given me what I needed.

A couple of minutes to go and I so hoped we'd get just a little bit more, something else to reward the months and months of work that I had put in. Jeremy raised his eyebrow again. 'You know what people think, they think, Paul Flowers, Methodist minister, how on earth does that happen? How does he end up involved with rent boys and drugs, he's a Methodist minister!' Flowers seemed annoyed. He was determined to keep up his schtick – that he was the victim here somehow, incapable of expressing genuine and meaningful remorse. 'And they have not had to live in my skin,' he responded. 'They have not bothered to enquire about the other pressures which were upon my life. And I would not wish to talk with them about them because they clearly hold me in complete contempt.'

Jeremy let him expand on his theme: 'Do you want to talk about these other pressures in your life?' Here, again, was new information, and Flowers jumped at the chance to blame other factors for his behaviour. 'At the time when things were getting pretty hairy at the bank, I had been caring for my mother at home, who was dying, with everything else that was going on, I was weary and stressed, not least at seeing somebody who I loved die in front of me. And it took a long time. But I would not want to use that as an excuse, it simply happens to be part of the reality that I was facing, and which is common to lots of people.'

Jeremy wasn't convinced. 'But most of us don't resort to drugs and rent boys.' Flowers gave his first brilliant reply: 'How do you know?'

As anticipated, the 'I'm a sinner' line took off, and was all over the news and the papers. This is the true mark of an interview being a success. The more that he damned himself, the better the outcome for us. He'd done a lot to make his situation even worse. It wasn't that I didn't feel any human empathy for him, just not the same kind that you'd feel for someone more blameless. You'd make your own judgements about who 'deserved' to get a hard time. And who didn't. Perhaps that's not a line most people are willing to draw, but I am. For me he was firmly in the former camp. His job and his actions necessitated greater scrutiny. He had agreed to do the interview, and there would be consequences – good and bad. That's the risk he took.

Much to my delight, the *Mail on Sunday* dedicated four whole pages to analysing and critiquing the interview. This was satisfying for me. That kind of coverage from our fiercest critic. 'Flower's brazen TV lies', the headline read, 'a simpering Paxman and a shameful new low for the "impartial" BBC: Furious backlash after BBC let Left-wing Methodist lie.' And then they used that word that kicks any booker in the teeth: they called the interview 'soft'.

Of course, people in the office were furious. But I knew that they were largely right, and it made me uncomfortable. That seemingly imperceptible change in Paxman, that lack of bite, that indifference, had been there for them to see too.

And then, just a few days later, it all made sense. The office had an awkward energy that only comes when bad news is pending: hushed conversations, important executives strode in and out, looking like they were doing 'important work'. Ian looked pleased. Something was awry.

Ian called a team meeting. The head of news, James Harding, showed up. Paxman walked wearily towards the centre of the office, with an air of surrender. We all gathered around, silent, expectant, fearful. They announced that, after twenty-five years at the helm, Jeremy had decided he was leaving. He'd be gone in two months.

I burst into tears. I can't say it was my most professional moment, but I like to think that Jeremy appreciated the sentiment.

The rest of the office was silent, many of them in shock, as we mulled over what this might mean for the programme, for us, for the future of how to conduct 'the interview'. The tension between these two men seemed to have come to a head. And the Editor had won.

If Paxman, with his illustrious career, was leaving, it was going to be even harder for me to stay.

The Paul Flowers interview was my last with Jeremy. Both of those men had lost their jobs. Mine? Hanging on by a thread.

4

Broken Blonde: Mel Greig

Two years. That's the longest I spent pursuing a single interview. And it was worth it.

It isn't sustainable to keep pursuing every lead. There simply wouldn't be time for other work. Every now and again I would do a cost benefit analysis on some of the long-term ones, and many would drop off my list. Some because the potential interviewees were so adamant that they didn't want to do it that ultimately I had to believe them; some because they would drop out of the news and become less relevant. But others get into your psyche, and you cannot give up.

One of those was the 'Royal Hoax Call DJ'. I can still remember the call – it caused a sensation. This was in 2012, when Twitter, and the social media culture we now take for granted, was only beginning. And the recorded call, dubbed 'the easiest prank call ever made', to the Lindo Wing at St Mary's Hospital in Paddington, went truly viral.

It was, for starters, the perfect prank. It was the kind of thing that other people were jealous of, wishing they had thought of it, wishing it had been their joke. But it quickly took a very dark turn. Lives were ruined. And at its centre was the Australian radio DJ Mel Greig.

She and her co-host, a seldom-mentioned man called Michael Christian, made the fateful call at 5.30 a.m. on Tuesday 4 December 2012. At the time, the Duchess of Cambridge was at St Mary's Hospital, being cared for during a hideous bout of extreme morning sickness. The duo called the hospital and somehow convinced a nurse not only that they were the Queen and Prince Charles but also, more crucially, to release some private medical information about the Duchess – hugely embarrassing for all parties concerned. Worst of all, after checking on the Duchess's health, the pretend Queen, Mel Greig, was actually put through to her hospital room. The ruse was only spotted by the Duchess's staff after one of the DJs made enquiries about various corgis on the call. Then they finally hung up. The call was broadcast a day later, on 5 December. It was the perfect outcome for the DJs and a humiliating lapse of protocol for the hospital.

Of course, such a prank could have passed without serious repercussion, being forgotten days, maybe weeks, later – after demands for hospitals to tighten up their procedures, or after some public apology by the trust's chief executive. But, tragically, the nurse who had picked up the phone killed herself. Jacintha Saldanha was forty-six. She had two children. A dedicated and experienced night nurse, she hadn't released any information about the Duchess, that detail was given by someone else, but she'd transferred that fateful call and had rued her part in it all, despite the hospital, and the Royal Family, putting no blame on her. She was found dead at the hospital nurses' accommodation on 7 December 2012.

Instantly, everything changed. Amusement turned to global condemnation. Mel Greig – a striking blonde in her thirties – did a tear-soaked TV apology, and the cycle started all over again. Now her remorse was vilified, her regrets despised, her apologies met with scorn and threats of violence. The same people who had, no doubt, laughed, now wanted her sacked, punished. She faced a deluge of the special sort of vitriol reserved for women in the public eye. Years of vicious trolling ensued. Greig would later admit contemplating suicide.

I remember it vividly because I wasn't used to seeing that kind of public shaming back then, particularly towards ordinary professional women. You could see the celebrity circus in full swing, with the daily coverage of the love lives of Madonna or Britney Spears, and the endless interest in their latest meltdown or spat, but you had to be *really* well known to get that kind of attention. News outlets were limited – you could buy *News of the World* or a celebrity gossip magazine, but the 24/7 culture of content hadn't yet taken full force. There just wasn't the direct access to people that we take for granted today. It seems naïve to say it now – in our daily cycle of rape threats and death threats and trial by social media. But, back then, the vilification seemed interminable in a way I hadn't seen before. It was unrelenting. Greig had nowhere to escape. Of course, it was horrific that Jacintha had died, appalling that these two poor children had lost their mother, a husband had lost his wife, but there was something so primal about the hatred that Greig in particular had unleashed. It was one of the moments that led to today's culture of trial by Twitter populated by anonymous and enraged keyboard warriors.

Things moved fast – the radio station, Sydney's 2Day FM, issued an apology, as did Greig and Christian, but, while he stayed on air, she decided to leave the station.

She started legal action against the station, saying the workplace wasn't safe for her to work in. He decided to remain, was back on air after his initial suspension, and his career continued. Months later, Christian won an internal competition and was named 'Next Top Jock', something that has since been deemed in bad taste. But Greig was unemployed and an instant industry pariah.

When I read that Mrs Saldanha had taken her own life, I started trying to contact Greig. She wasn't following me on Twitter, so I had to go via her agent. Unsurprisingly her agent was inundated with requests for interviews with Greig. I can only imagine how overwhelmed she must have been when she declined mine.

But I had a resolute, even deluded, refusal to take 'no' for an answer. It's what I like to think distinguished me from other bookers. I could barely believe it when I later discovered that some people in my position try to find an email address for someone, maybe send a message on Twitter, leave a voicemail that's never returned, and then move on. It's only ever 1% of the time that you get an immediate 'yes'; the other 99% is about painstaking, persistent, charming, deliberate, incessant pursuit. Little by little, without me ever knowing it, other producers would forget to try again, get distracted by some new newsworthy person, lose conviction, while I would endure.

Meanwhile Mel Greig's agent endured my email entreaties for almost two years. In that time, I watched everything that Mel did, believed her regret to be genuine, and tried to find what would be a tipping point that would finally get her to agree to speak with us. My bid was twofold: firstly, that the tragedy had happened here in the UK and that she owed the family of Mrs Saldanha, the British public, the Royal Family, an explanation of her behaviour, and an apology in person; and, secondly, that until that was done, she would not be able to move on emotionally.

For months and months the answer still came back as a firm 'no'. But then, in 2014, something changed – Mel announced that she would attend Mrs Saldanha's London inquest. She wasn't specifically required to attend or to say anything, but she had clearly decided it was the right thing to do, to make herself available. She tweeted: 'I made a commitment to the Saldanha family that I would answer any questions they have, on or off the stand,' and I knew this was my chance. Just like that, she felt the same way – the two years of 'no' became 'yes'. She would give us her first ever UK interview.

By now, things were a little different on *Newsnight*. Paxman had been gone for a few months, and in his place was Evan Davis. Evan is a pleasure to work with – easy-going, well prepared, clever and calm, but, to my mind, a totally different type of interviewer. Gone were the expectations of interrogation, and instead he'd brought in a more discursive, gentle style, designed to elicit information through calm persistence rather than antagonism. Ian Katz had just done an interview in the *Financial Times* about the change in approach – titled 'The death of the political interview'. The comment piece didn't even try to avoid taking a swipe at Paxman, and seemed like a justification for his demise, commenting, 'For the most part interviews with frontbenchers are an arid, ritualised affair . . .' Then followed a long critique of that 'aggressive style characterised by the dictum "Why is this lying bastard lying to me?"' And so it went on . . .

I can see why many people like the gentler style but, for me, it was not the right fit for what we did best – interviews around accountability with politicians and heads of state. In those interviews we seek to address something crucial – the democratic deficit. We solicit answers to the questions that our viewers deserve to know. We're not bothered about whether a politician feels comfortable. We're holding them to account – finding the flaws in their reasoning – and this *ought* to make them uncomfortable. Being able to justify themselves comes with the territory. It is what their electorate, and the BBC viewer, deserves.

That robustness was the very thing that brought me into *Newsnight*; the thought of its dilution depressed me. Without it, I couldn't see what exactly the programme offered that was special and unique.

Conversely, Evan's demeanour would be perfect for this kind of interview – with a weary and injured woman, who had taken years of vile online abuse, and who had never done a UK broadcast interview before. She would need his style of solicitous coaxing to tell her story.

The Editor was delighted with my 'get' and I set about making the logistical arrangements. 'Getting' the interview is only a small part of the task – next there's the logistics, taxis, hotel, travel, hair, make-up, cameras, lights, snacks; it's all part of the producer's job to make sure each element is in place. And there's always the fear that someone will back out, change their mind, lose their mettle. In this particular interview it seemed far more likely than most to end that way. Added to that, the announcement that Greig was coming to London had thrown the tabloid media into a frenzy. She had featured prominently on the front pages for weeks in 2012 and now, in 2014, she was front page news all over again. It seems the media couldn't get enough of this young, broken, photogenic blonde.

The first picture I remember of a 'female blonde victim' was that of Rachel Nickell. She was murdered on

Wimbledon Common in 1992, while out walking with her two-year-old son. We interviewed him years later, another 'exclusive' for the programme. But it was her image – twenty-three, white, blonde, smiling, carefree – that was the front page for weeks. It stayed with me for years. The coverage these sorts of women attracted – whether dead or alive – would obliterate all others. Countless other victims, black, Asian, middle-aged, got a fraction of the coverage. The image of the young blonde Madeleine McCann still appears at each twist in her tragic tale. Some victims make it into the papers endlessly. Others do not. As time went on, we became more aware of the kinds of decisions we, the media, took about this. The omissions and prejudices that those decisions revealed weren't random.

As every headline hit, I became jumpier and jumpier that she'd back out of our agreement and so it was decided that, when she arrived, I would stay with her all day. In part to keep the paparazzi at bay and to protect the integrity of our exclusive.

It was my ideal kind of day. I love spending time with prospective interviewees. Of course, the finished product is everything to the team and to the news machine but, to me, the experience itself, the person in the flesh, the off-camera details they share, the proximity to them, is the best part of the job. To spend most of the day in her company, to try and reassure, calm, help, but also to discuss in private what had happened to her since that December call, was a privilege. I'd seen her life unfold in print and on screen for two years and now I would get six hours without any apparatus.

Her hotel was only a couple of streets away from the BBC. It was one of those old-fashioned London buildings that you pass every day, but never notice, tucked down a side street, with an entrance that looks like a private home. It felt unchanged since the 1970s – dark wallpaper, dark lighting, a musty smell and carpets that had seen better days. I was met with some suspicion by the hotel receptionist, even though she knew I was coming, and we'd hired a nearby basement room to conduct the interview. There's often a default mistrust of 'journalists' and she eyed me warily, reluctantly checking if she was allowed to send me up to Mel's room. I was directed to one of the musty chairs, like a naughty schoolchild, and waited, expectantly, for her to grant me the permission to go upstairs. She was clearly enjoying her two-minute power trip.

The lift squeaked in protest at my presence. I breathed deeply as I approached Mel's room. The mustiness of the corridor entered my lungs. I knew that if she lost her nerve, not only would two years of work be wasted, but the blame would be laid firmly at my feet, and I couldn't afford another setback.

As Mel opened the door, I noticed we weren't completely dissimilar. Although she was a decade younger, we both wore tight trousers and high heels, with long blonde hair and make-up aplenty. The hair and make-up artist had arrived before me (essential for most TV shoots) and the contents of her metal suitcase of foundations, lipsticks and eye shadows littered the bed. Mel broke into a warm smile, extended her hand and led me inside.

The detritus of getting 'camera-ready' was every-where. Mel's hair was in curlers and it was being tousled and pulled and styled to the nth degree. Clothes were scattered on the floor. The make-up artist and she had a good rapport and were laughing and smiling, albeit Mel's nervousness pervaded the room. It had the atmos-phere of a teen slumber party – laced with the heavy inevitability of the interview. Though Mel was never tricky or demanding in any way, her demeanour was that of someone who was clearly defeated and scared but was trying to make the best of it. The three of us did so together – sharing stories about our personal lives, fash-ion tips, London bar recommendations and chatting about every kind of triviality we could find. It wasn't that she was a trivial person – she was clearly clever and empathetic and kind – but it was the only way to evade the conversation neither of us wanted to have – about what she would go through later that day and how, quite possibly, this visit and this interview would serve to stoke up the relentless attention that she had carried for so long. It was a fake teen slumber party. It wasn't fun or congenial, it was a distraction. But we both went through the motions – discussing make-up instead of suicides. It was about creating an atmosphere that kept her as upbeat as possible. You're always looking for that commonality, as there's such a brief time in which to establish a rapport. Sometimes it'd be something to do with my background, education, profession or interests – this time, it was make-up and fashion.

I can't confirm whether her life had been ruined by what happened, but it certainly felt like it. Some of the consequences are well documented – the end of a relationship and a career brought to a premature end. Some were more personal; she speculated that her failure to have a child served as a fateful comeuppance for depriving two children of their mother. She was a broken woman. And her regret was gut-wrenchingly sincere. Some interviewees go through the motions, more or less convincingly. Not Mel. She struck me as a woman who knew the true horror of what had happened and would carry it with her to her dying day.

The hours ebbed away, and we came closer and closer to Evan's arrival. Eventually, we had to leave behind the cheery mess of make-up and clothes to face the harsh lights of the basement room, which had been set up in the interim. The change in atmosphere was palpable. All geniality disappeared. I led Mel to her fate – beneath the cruel, hot lights of the airless room.

She looked so small, so scared, so young. Her outfit – a white blazer with an embroidered black chevron pattern on the shoulders and arms, a black T-shirt, a locket in the shape of a heart, her hair, her make-up – suddenly jarred. Evan arrived – all smart suit, polished shoes, shirt and tie – and the contrast was even starker. She asked for some water. She gulped. The cameraman positioned some bright flowers to the right of her head, and we all waited for the interview to start. Because the logistics – putting on a microphone, checking the cameras are in focus, that the sound is working – take a few minutes, the presenter's rapport with an interviewee becomes crucial. Evan is great at this. Sensing her tension, he passed niceties, smiled, reassured her, thanked her for coming, and the moments of technicalities passed. It was time to start. The cameras were ready to roll. Mel looked at me one last time. She swallowed again. I copied her.

Evan smiled, and asked his first question. 'Do you regret making that call?' Mel looked ashen by this point, and exhaled. 'It never should have been suggested, we never should have called a hospital. And that's in hindsight, but when we went to call the hospital, we didn't think about any kind of consequences, because you think you're calling a media centre, you think that there's going to be someone there that's been fielding these prank calls all day, and it did come out at the inquest that there were other prank calls that day. People were calling the hospital, and we stupidly thought people would be there to field those calls.' Her cheeks were flushed.

By contrast, Evan looked cool and collected. He also had a bouquet in shot, to the left of his head, but his aura was that of someone doing something simple, something inconsequential, while Mel was on trial for her life. He fixed her with his calm stare and asked, 'Where were you, what were you doing, when you heard the news about Jacintha?' Her tone dropped and she spoke slowly, deliberately. 'I was in bed. It was about midnight in Australia, and my partner was on Twitter. And he saw all these tweets coming through saying "you have blood on your hands", "you are responsible for the nurse's death", and he couldn't quite understand where these tweets were coming from and why. And I was woken up and found out.' The cameraman took the opportunity to zoom in on Mel's face, to gauge her reaction. 'I went into complete shock. I was hysterical. As I'm sure the Saldanha family were. And that's where my thoughts were straight away – with how they'd be coping with it.' She stared blankly ahead.

Evan looked even more relaxed, his chin rested on his hand; he was engaged and listening to her responses carefully. A presenter maintains a hugely important professional distance to allow the forensic and impartial questioning that follows. They keep a barrier between them and the person in the chair, they are fleeting acquaintances. By contrast, I share an intimacy with the people we interview, who I sometimes spend hours and hours speaking with, whose lives I know in far more detail than the interviews ever reveal, and my relationships with them are often not fleeting. Long after the presenter has left for their next appointment, I will often still be there, talking to the interviewee, or their representative, taking their questions, dealing with their concerns. We usually stay in touch, while the presenter usually never speaks to them again. The contrast in this situation was stark.

Evan continued, 'Looking back on it, should you feel guilty about that prank? I know this is a question a lot of people have asked, isn't it? There's no way you could have really anticipated that outcome, and yet, clearly, it was perhaps a trigger, or one trigger of several, leading to Jacintha Saldanha's terrible state of mind over the next few days.'

This was Mel's chance to apologise. And she took it. 'People handle things differently as well. For me? Instant guilt and blame for the next eighteen to twenty months. And I will always always feel at fault to an extent, because I was on that prank call, and I was mentioned in Jacintha's suicide note. Not "The Australian DJ", but my name. She thought of me before she took her own life, how can you not feel guilty and blame, and I always will, but I have learnt to deal with it now.' There was a sharp intake of breath in the room at that detail. Perhaps we had forgotten, perhaps it had passed us by, but to be specifically named in Jacintha's suicide note. An unimaginable punishment.

After Mrs Saldanha's death, 2Day FM took a huge amount of criticism. They had tried, but failed, so they said, to get the relevant permissions to air the call, and so had run it anyway, without anything that would identify the nurses they spoke to, but with enough detail to let the world know what had happened. Whether that should have happened remained contentious for months and months. Long after Mel had left the station. And there'd even been calls to end this kind of, mostly, harmless fun. Evan asked Mel what she thought of that: 'You wouldn't take the view that there shouldn't be radio programmes of this kind, or would you take that view?'

Mel paused before replying. 'In fact, I think we need to make sure the joke is on us. If you're thinking of doing a prank, or a stunt or even commenting on something on air or writing a comment to someone online, think how it's going to affect the other person. If you don't know them, if you don't know how they can handle it, don't do it. You just have to look out for each other. That's what we need to do – we need to be mindful of other people's mental state and how it might affect them.'

This seems like such an obvious thing to say now, almost a decade after the call, but it was a relatively new idea at the time. As broadcasters, as journalists, as individuals, we were grappling with the duality of social media. Of course, it was an extraordinary opportunity for content and journalism to reach countless people across the world, but it was also a new relationship with viewers and with the consumers. They could connect with and criticise us publicly all day long. I was used to facing reproach about the BBC, and its various flaws, in my 'real' life, but suddenly, even as producers, we were subject to a whole new onslaught, and an expectation of accountability, far beyond that of the licence fee payers themselves. I've had it easy – with a small number of Twitter followers and a low profile, exchanges about what I posted were largely friendly, appreciative or congenial. There were no consequences if I blocked someone who was rude or disrespectful. But, for presenters like Evan and, later, Emily Maitlis, the beast of social media created countless challenges. It created challenges for perceptions about their impartiality, a new public arena to make accidental factual mistakes that could be repeated and criticised for weeks, and, mostly for the female presenters, a place to endure relentless comments about their appearance. It's the reason I most enjoy being behind the camera, out of the public eye. I would hate that kind of attention.

Mel Greig had faced the online assault for years. 'You just need to, we have to look out for each other, you cannot take the risk that someone's mental health is going to be able to handle that. If you don't know them and you've played this horrible prank or this horrible joke, you can't, you just can't do it!' Her voice rose, and, for a moment, I thought she might cry. But she gathered herself, exhaled, and prepared herself for the next question.

Evan continued, 'The genesis of the joke, whose idea was it?' This one struck fear into my heart. It's the corollary of not getting credit when things go right, that a producer may also evade getting the heat when they go wrong. I had assumed there was someone else on the team who had come up with this plan – I can imagine one of us thinking it was a great idea, congratulating ourselves, then being devastated by the outcome. Mel wasn't going to shift the blame, though.

'I don't want to name names,' she replied, 'because I don't want to put another individual through what I have been through. It's disgusting and I don't want them to be trolled, to be harassed, and a whole new witch hunt. It was a member of the team, but we were all in agreeance, so it's not about individuals, we were all in agreeance, and not for a second did we think "that's a terrible idea" because you don't expect to get through to nurses. I still can't understand why nurses are answering the phones. And I don't want to put the blame on the hospital at all, I'm here to take absolute responsibility, but I also think hospitals should look into their procedures and policies.'

Evan was doing a good job. His style was not only different to Paxman's, but to most of the women present-ers I worked with too. The cliché is that women are more empathetic when interviewing and, largely, I've found that to be true. Kirsty Wark, Emma Barnett, Emily Maitlis, Mishal Husain, they'd all have done it differently. I'm not sure if it's nature or nurture, but you'll tend to feel more humanity between two women. Or, if they don't connect, more animosity. It's not better, or worse, it's just different. Evan's style was much more that of a curious and interested professional. He was asking to elicit information. He wasn't seeking the kind of commonality or bond I traded in.

Evan returned to the crux of the issue – what was it like to be both the perpetrator of an internet sensation turned tragedy, but also to be the victim of it turning against you? 'Tell me how it feels to be on the end of that?' Mel paused. 'Look, when I think about this, all I think about is the Saldanha family and how hard it was for them, so I don't want to sit here and go "poor me, it was terrible" because they've lost a wife and a mother. But the trolling and the death threats were disgusting. You know, I was in lockdown for months. There were bullets with our names on it sent to police stations . . .'

That was our headline: 'Bullets in the post.'

Mel continued, '. . . and the turning point for me, the difference between an opinion and a troll, was when someone wrote to me and then rang my mother and said, "Eye for an eye, you deserve to die." ' At this stage, she finally cracked. Her face turned red, her cheeks began to glow, her eyes glistened with tears brimming over; she turned her face away from the camera's glare, her expression full of pain. 'When you bring my mother into it and I didn't want to cry but it's just – that's the difference, and that's unnecessary.'

One of the things about the whole affair that interested me the most was that issue of how different the outcomes had been for Mel and her colleague, Michael Christian. Mel was the pariah; she didn't work for years after the incident while he was suspended for a short stint but then stayed on air and was later given that 'Top Jock' prize. She was extremely memorable. I couldn't even remember what he looked like. The line between criticising the fascination with her and enabling it ourselves was blurry. Our own coverage would return the gaze to her. We'd be starting a whole new cycle of attention. We were complicit, even if we didn't want to see it that way.

Evan addressed the gender discrepancy. 'It seems like it's been much tougher on you than on your colleague Mike Christian, who was also involved in the joke, because he's been working as a DJ, he's been acclaimed, he's won awards. He does seem to have moved on. What's the difference, why has it been easier on him, do you think?'

I could see Mel didn't want to fall into the trap of moving the blame onto him, but it stuck in her craw. Any of us in the media knows the difference in the treatment men and women can get online, and, even in those early days, it was apparent. She evaded putting any blame on him, but tackled that issue head on. 'It's mental health, people really do handle things differently. He was able to move forward, which is fantastic if he can do that, and he's not a bad person, he's really not, but he chose to stay with the company, and I chose to leave. So we are going down two completely different paths. I didn't know if I wanted to return to media, I certainly couldn't step foot back in that station, so, for me, it was just a whole different mind-set. And the media just seemed fixated on me. They would make my face the front page of the newspapers, trolls would target me, I don't know why, I don't know whether it was because I was female, but everything just seemed to be directed at me.'

Of course, we all knew that that hoax call would be something that defined her forever, that she would never be able to move away from it. This was her 'fifteen minutes of fame' gone horribly wrong.

Her final words acknowledged this, laced with both anger and resignation. 'I actually have a real name, it's Mel, it's not "Royal Hoax DJ". But that's now who I am, and it follows me everywhere, and it's tarnished me, and people just know me as "the Royal Hoax DJ". I worked in radio for fifteen years, it was my dream job that I'd worked so hard to get. But now I am "the Royal Hoax DJ" and that's horrible.'

The conversation ended. The cameras stopped rolling. Evan had his mic removed and left for his next assignment. Mel disentangled herself from the various wires, left the glare of the lights, gathered her possessions, went back to her murky hotel room.

The exchange moved viewers and the line about 'bullets in the post' ran all across the country. To this day, my pursuit of that interview is used in BBC training for new journalists – as an example of the kind of determination and persistence it takes to get exclusive content.

Mel and I remain in touch. She managed to rebuild her career, works as an advocate against cyber-bullying and even made it onto *The Celebrity Apprentice Australia*.

She is still blonde, beautiful and hopefully a little less broken.

5

Women and Girls:
Gina and Amanda

'I need police!' The girl's voice on the 911 call was desperate, frightened, broken. 'OK, and what's going on there?' the operator asked. Her reply was breathless: 'I've been kidnapped, and I've been missing for ten years, and I'm here!'

For over a decade, there was a dark secret hidden away in Cleveland, Ohio. In a quiet suburb, three girls were imprisoned, tortured, beaten and raped. The three girls – who became women in captivity – were Michelle Knight, Amanda Berry and Gina DeJesus. Ariel Castro, a school bus driver, had kidnapped all three between 2002 and 2004. Michelle was the first at twenty-one, Amanda, sixteen, in 2003, and the youngest, Gina, just fourteen, in

2004. The younger two were school friends of Castro's daughter, Arlene. And together they languished in his basement. Later, he moved them to barricaded rooms upstairs. Throughout their confinement, the young women were subjected to unspeakable acts of sexual violence and degradation.

The house was unassuming, typical to the area. 2207 Seymour Avenue, Tremont, Ohio. The grey concrete steps led to a little outside space, where, no doubt, Castro whiled away his evenings. White wooden slats covered its exterior, four windows at the front, a pointed roof, a tiny sparse patch of grass in front of the porch, a small tree in the middle of the yard. Ten feet away on either side were other houses, spaced as such down the length of the street. A large tree stood in the middle of the pavement that had seen better days.

Castro was of average height and build, with olive skin and a receding hairline. He lived a seemingly mundane life. He continued his work as a school bus driver, ferrying kids across town. He played guitar in a local band and had family members over to the house. Eventually, he lost his job for making an illegal U-turn, leaving a kid aboard while he had lunch, grocery shopping on company time and leaving the bus unattended while he had a nap at home. Minor infractions, while the three young women spent a combined thirty years locked up. Until 6 May 2013, when they finally escaped.

As soon as they were found, they became celebrities. The story ran across every network, national and international, and the unbearableness of their experience was compounded by the distasteful, incessant glare of the media. They were overnight stars. Expected to do press conferences, newspaper interviews, give detailed accounts of the horror. From a circus of brutality to a circus of attention.

One of them, Amanda Berry, had managed to keep a diary of her experiences, of the abuse, and also of the day-to-day banalities. Publishers scrambled for it. And when it was announced that a book was coming out, co-authored with Gina, the youngest of the three, I found myself just as curious as everyone else.

I admit, with some shame, that I am as gripped by dark tales as I am comforted by hopeful endings. Their stories haunted and fascinated me. Most women are aware if not afraid of what a man can do to them against their will. Stories of abduction strike at the heart of female anxiety. As a journalist, I couldn't imagine a more purposeful interview – to give these women an opportunity to speak for themselves and for us to see beyond the sordid sexual element that the media were most obsessed by.

When a book like this comes out it's basically a bunfight between broadcasters to get the first interview, the heady 'exclusive'. Most Editors will only accept content if it's with the first interview, or, if they really want it, the first television interview, after a radio one. So, you can 'get' the interview, only to have it rejected because it's too far down the pecking order. The 'first broadcast' is the holy grail.

There is an assumption that when you get an interview pegged to a book, it's been fairly easy to achieve. Quite the opposite – usually competition is fiercer since everyone knows the individual will actually *want* the spotlight. So, each new book led me to mount a one-woman campaign for a high-value tender. I would respond to the first email within seconds, followed up by a phone call to show my basic interest, and to gauge whether the book publicist had a television slot, and who they might be minded to give it to. If we weren't knocked out straight away (sometimes I would be told 'We definitely won't be doing *Newsnight*' within seconds) then I would move on to the next stage. Research. The challenge I would always face was that, despite the profile of the programme, *Newsnight*'s viewing figures are far below Radio 4's *Today* programme (which is our direct competitor). Added to that, the programme's reputation for hostility would be a real hindrance, especially in delicate interviews of this kind. And so, I'd make sure my research was meticulous, to try to mitigate the handicaps we faced.

The first question to ask is, 'What would motivate these young women to choose us over everyone else?' And then, 'What would motivate the publicist to choose us when the world's media is clamouring at their door?' In this case, I felt we had some crucial advantages. Although many people prefer the ease of a radio interview – easy to do, zero focus on how you look, little equipment, over in minutes – in this case it felt like an important opportunity for Amanda and Gina to give their version of events for posterity, 'in vision' (filmed) and definitively. I knew they'd only do one interview.

We also had a secret weapon – Kirsty Wark. Kirsty is one of the kindest, most compassionate and decent people I have ever worked with. And she's brilliant at handling delicate content. Her style is never aggressive or cruel or prurient – it's patient and respectful. She had the best chance of eliciting the thoughtful and honest responses that these two women deserved to get the chance of giving. She would afford them the dignity and compassion they had been stripped of for years in captivity.

I composed my pitch. Sometimes this would take me a day to get right. Honing the tone, perfecting the wording, changing the emphasis, re-reading to get a sense of whether I, in someone else's shoes, might be tempted. If you were very lucky (about 1% of the time), you'd get a straightforward 'yes' back. But mostly, it'd be a generic 'thank you' email, and then a painful few weeks, or months, waiting for the final decision to be made. Hoping that you'd done enough to convince them, calibrating the offer when it was queried, chasing it gently every week (diarised, never missed). The other thing I had on my side this time was that the interest in this particular scoop was so huge that one of the BBC's documentary programmes, *Our World*, was keen to do a full half-hour version of the interview. Usually, programmes within the BBC are competing for content. This one time, we were going to offer a collaboration. In theory we are meant to collaborate a lot – makes sense for the public purse, good to share resources – but the atmosphere between programmes is rarely like that. It's far more contentious. Ultimately there's one winner and many losers. It seems nonsensical to outsiders, but that's the dynamic. On this occasion, if I landed the interview, *Our World* would go out after us and so it was a real added incentive for the book publicist to agree – forty-five minutes of prime BBC airtime.

I waited and waited.

The new Deputy Editor – a clever, calm, innovative bloke called Rob Burley – was equally excited. We both knew this would be a potential award winner, and compelling viewing. His enthusiasm was palpable, and it was nice to finally feel I had an ally on the team. I didn't think I was going to get sacked anymore but I certainly didn't feel at ease in my role. Although we never openly discussed it, Rob had my back and was cheerleading my successes. It was something I hadn't experienced for a long time.

Finally, we heard back. It was good news. I called Rob straight away. He was ecstatic, and we set about working out the logistics. In a case like this, where the interviewees were still young and vulnerable, getting every little part of the shoot right was crucial. We discussed whether Kirsty should call them personally beforehand, to break the ice and establish a rapport, but in the end we decided the best thing to do would be to arrange for Kirsty to arrive early and meet Amanda and Gina for a coffee or breakfast before going on air. Going on a trip like this is a real prize for a producer but, as ever, my personal circumstances didn't allow. Lucas was still young, and I was still unable to leave him. So, the lucky producer Rhoda Buchanan was chosen, Kirsty was updated, and all of us began working on the logistics and the brief.

By this stage the book had landed. I had to sign a non-disclosure agreement (NDA) before we received it and when it arrived – just one copy to start with – we had to guard it closely. The book had only been read by a handful of people around the world. The Diane Sawyer show, *ABC World News*, was going to speak with them first, in the US, but then we were the first international interview. Ever. If the NDA was broken, if contents of the book were leaked, we'd lose the interview instantly.

Often there wouldn't be time for me to read the book, but on this occasion I was determined to. I grabbed my new tome, left the office and holed myself up in a nearby bar. I knew the contents were going to be harrowing and so I ordered myself a drink. I needed it. Inside were the unrelenting horrors the girls had suffered, told through Amanda's diaries, and her series of codes for the acts she endured. 2x. 3x. 4x. That was her code for the number of rapes she'd endured on a given day. I read the whole book and was determined that an interview would look beyond these details, would do the women justice.

The team were due to fly to Ohio for the interview one week before it would air. That gave editors ample time to get it ready. But it was going to be a challenging trip and there was a lot to do to get a *Newsnight* piece and a documentary done in that time frame. As a backup, we had a very experienced award-winning producer in London,

Nick Blakemore, who could get involved if it all became too much.

Kirsty and Rhoda left for Ohio. Rob and I waited behind.

When the team returned, days later, it was clear something special had taken place. I wasn't sure how well the women would respond to the intensity and trauma of having to relive the ordeal, but I'd hoped they had been able to say what they wanted. Amanda was articulate, open, mesmerising. Gina was no less spellbinding, though she struggled to speak at times.

Here were two self-possessed adults. Amanda, straight blonde hair tied into a neat ponytail, was dressed in a conservative black top, with a white collar and white button detail. Formal, smart, chic. To her left, the more visibly nervous Gina, with brown, slightly wavy bobbed hair, wearing a bright orange dress, short sleeved, and a cheerful blue and green scarf hung loosely around her neck. The room was cosy, like an older relative's house, peppered with slightly dated personal items. Along with the usual array of colourful flowers, a dark mahogany side table filled the void between their chairs. It was adorned with various blurry accoutrements – a random old book, a pen jar, some desk lamps. Finally, behind Amanda, there was a bookcase, full of dusty volumes that looked like they would be on academic reading lists, but were all too out of focus to discern.

Kirsty sat, calm and composed, wearing a simple black dress, glasses and a necklace. She knew that it was important to wear something that wouldn't be distracting or discordant with the day's work. As ever, the wardrobe choices women make on screen would be scrutinised. Just as Gina and Amanda would have decided upon their attire to look 'smart' or to feel comfortable, the same decisions would have been made by Kirsty too. She'd have considered what her clothes communicated, whether they were too imposing on the scene and its sombre nature. Probably discussed it with the producer. Contemplated it together. Things that shouldn't matter. But they still do. Hopefully one day they won't.

Amanda spoke first. 'I had gotten off work early that day, and I worked at Burger King. I had called my sister for a ride, she was at work, and I had called a friend for a ride, and he didn't answer, so I just started walking and, as I was walking there was a van, and it was in a driveway that I had to go around. I looked up and saw a man and a girl in a van. The girl looked like someone that I had worked with and so I smiled at them, continued to walk. A couple of minutes later the van pulls up and he says, "Do you need a ride?"'

In that van was Ariel Castro. Who knows how long he had planned to take her – he'd already had one captive, Michelle, in his house for a year. How long had he been watching her? Or was the meeting random and the act spontaneous? As any grown woman knows, we live with the burden of expectation that *some* harm will be done to us at *some* stage. At the time, Amanda thought nothing of it. She was on her way home, without a care. 'I had my Burger King outfit on so he noticed that and he was talking about how his son had used to work there and that I knew a couple of his kids so . . .' 'So it was kind of a casual conversation?' 'Yes.' The next minute, she was in the van. Just like that, she was gone.

Kirsty said, 'And then of course, when you get to the house, you immediately know that he's not going to let you out?' Amanda looked intently at Kirsty. 'Yes,' she said and nodded.

When she arrived, he took her into a bedroom. It was dark, and he didn't turn on the lights. Once she was inside, she knew she was in trouble. His daughter, who he'd said was inside, was nowhere to be seen. And then, he told her to pull down her knickers. She screamed for help which never came. Very quickly, she was chained to a pole and left, alone, in that dark room, with only a television for company. She thought she was going to die. A decade of her life was about to be stolen from her.

Amanda had just celebrated her sixteenth birthday when she was kidnapped. When she was captive in Castro's house, she discovered his first victim – twenty-one-year-old Michelle Knight. He now had two victims. Neither was allowed out.

A year later, Gina was taken. She was fourteen. Her recollection was filled with the quiet emotion of that day. 'I was walking home from school, with his daughter Arlene Castro, and she used the payphone to call her mom, to ask her if she could come to my house, and her mom said no, she went her other way and I went the other way. He asked me if I had seen his daughter, and I said "yes". And he was like, "can you help me find her?", and I was like, "yes". And then he didn't turn around and we ended up going to his house.'

The same technique. The same outcome.

He had now taken two of his daughter's friends. Two of her social group. Destroyed the lives of families that she knew, traumatised the community. The girls lived for a decade on Seymour Avenue, less than four miles from where they were abducted. Ariel Castro had moved there in 1992. He remained there for over twenty years, until Amanda escaped in 2013.

The girls lived, chained, with a bucket for a bathroom, in separate rooms, but just feet away from one another.

Amanda in one room, Gina and Michelle in another. Gina described it to Kirsty, her face ashen. 'Well, my chain went through her wall to my wall, like through a wall, because her room and my room were connected so it went straight through a wall, and then I'm like divided from my ankle to Michelle's ankle.'

Kirsty didn't make them relive every terrible detail, but it all had one thing in common – this man clearly took pleasure in their pain, enjoyment from their suffering. 'I think the more we cried and showed him our pain and our sorrow, like he got energy from that,' Amanda explained, 'it helped him, so we kinda learned, we learned, right? Just don't cry, don't show him your pain, don't show him you're mad.' She looked over at Gina, locked in their mutual understanding, both distraught. Gina just nodded very slowly.

Castro even interacted with Gina's family. Gina's parents, Nancy and Felix, never gave up the search for their missing daughter. One day, he did something even more heartless to Gina: he told her he had talked to her mum. He was on his motorcycle, and he had seen her handing out flyers about Gina's disappearance. He went up to Nancy, took one of the flyers and asked if there was any information about her disappearance. Obviously fishing to see what they knew. He gave Gina the flyer to keep, and she treasured it, because it was the only thing she had left of her family, and it made her feel close to them. She decorated it. Kept it. Looked at it. Kept hoping. 'Did you think that you'd be able to keep that flyer to the day that you saw her?' Kirsty asked. Gina mumbled a 'yes', almost inaudibly, and then looked down, and was silent.

On their TVs, the girls even saw their families making incessant pleas for information, keeping their stories alive. Amanda watched each news item with hope. 'You know, that was the only way we knew how they looked, what had changed within a year, to know that they were still fighting for you.' Those news stories kept her going.

In 2006, three years into Amanda's ordeal, something momentous happened: Amanda got pregnant. 'I had realised that I hadn't got my period, and that was like the first sign, and then I had started like getting sick, I couldn't eat anything, and I would just throw it up, and so that was the sign.' I was shocked. Amanda was pregnant the same year as I was, and at the exact same time. We were just two months apart. As my joyful pregnancy progressed, she wasn't even sure if hers would be permitted. As I went to the doctor, received scans, had a party to celebrate, decided which extraordinary medical care I would receive, she languished on that bedroom floor. While I bought a cot, did a birthing plan, researched nappies, she didn't even know if he would allow her to carry the baby to term. She knew he didn't want a baby in the house, 'because you know if the baby cries, or the neighbours hear a baby, or someone comes to the house, what do you do with a baby? How do you keep a baby quiet?' And she knew it was unlikely the baby would live. Michelle had been pregnant several times, the babies didn't make it. Each time he starved her and beat her so badly that she miscarried. Amanda had assumed the same fate for her child. But, by some miracle, he allowed the pregnancy to progress. Each day she feared it would be ended. Each day she hoped it wouldn't be.

That year, we both went into labour. For me, it was the middle of the night. My then husband and I packed my bag into the car and drove across Hammersmith, full of expectation and excitement, on my way to endless resources, pain-relief and care. For Amanda, in Ohio, the experience couldn't have been more different. 'I really didn't even know I was going into labour, I just had labour pains all day, but I had no idea what it was. Eventually, I had to use the bathroom, and I heard something pop and I didn't know what it was but then he's like "oh, I think your water broke", so he takes me upstairs into my bedroom, and he brings out this baby pool, and that's where I had to lay until I had the baby, so I didn't make a mess on the bed.' While I was waiting on a ward, my husband by my side, midwives and doctors bustling around me, Amanda only had her fellow captive to help. 'So he had gotten Michelle to come in and help me deliver the baby. And he sat in a rocking chair and read a baby book, about how to give birth.' Miraculously, the baby was delivered safely. She was healthy, she was allowed to live. My baby arrived also, but I wasn't in the same position, on this one thing. He was extremely ill, rushed to ICU, given a day to live. We were in a haze, told to expect to make funeral arrangements. Delirious with love and with the promise of grief. If that had been Amanda's baby, he wouldn't have made it. By some miracle of our own he made it. By some miracle of her own, Amanda's daughter made it too. Lucas and Jocelyn came into the world.

Side by side, our children grew. Mine in parks and playgroups, hers within the same four walls, day after day.

Eventually, the time came for going to school. Lucas went to his local nursery followed by the local community primary state school, Flora Gardens. We'd eat breakfast (Weetabix, milk, raspberries and banana), get dressed, walk there hand in hand, gathering leaves, looking at dogs, waving at friends. Jocelyn had a very different school of her own. A school that Amanda fashioned in that captivity. Her words broke my heart: 'We'd wake up in the morning, we would have breakfast, we would pretend-walk to school, yeah, I tried to make it as real as possible for her, you know, so we would lock the door, and we would walk to school, cross streets, and I would tell her, you know, stop at green lights and look both ways when it's a red light, and we would finally get to school and I would set her down and tell her, "OK, I love you, have a good day!" And then I would become her teacher!' It was a rare moment in the interview where she gave a truly warm smile and laughed with genuine joy. She was heroic. She was everything.

Amid the brutality, there were small moments of happiness. In 2011, eight years into her captivity, Amanda watched the wedding of Prince William and Kate Middleton. I was working that day and the newsroom was filled with wedding paraphernalia. One of my colleagues had brought some paper tiaras, another had some confetti, we were laughing and joking all day. I'd booked a stellar – and important – panel. Earl Spencer, Princess Diana's brother, agreed to come on. I'd also persuaded Martin Bashir, now in the US, still riding high on his Diana interview triumph.

Meanwhile, chained to the floor, thousands of miles away, Amanda observed the same scenes. 'It was like the biggest thing on all the news channels, you know, and I loved watching the news, to know what was going on in the world, and they're like well, you know, you have to wake up at 6 a.m. and it's going to be on this channel, and so I actually set my clock and got up at 6 a.m.! To me that was just something that would, I don't know, it's happiness, they're getting married, and to see what her dress looked like, and to see all the people there, it was just beautiful. I still one day want to get married and have a family. You know, that normalcy!' Kirsty asked her what she thought of the dress. Amanda laughed. 'I think it could have been a little fancier – she is a princess!'

Finally, in 2013, the day came that the three girls had always hoped for, against hope. And it was little Jocelyn, now six years old, who was their salvation. Unlike the three women, she was allowed to wander about the house. We all know that we'd do anything to give a tiny sense of normality to a child in a situation like that. Jocelyn knew nothing but imprisonment, she had no clue that her fate was a heinous one. She went from Mummy to Daddy, sometimes wandered about, now and again he'd even let her outside. Amanda described the day: 'So Jocelyn goes to go downstairs, because she was allowed to go downstairs, you know, when she wanted, if he had the door open usually. And so she goes downstairs, and she's, I guess, looking for him, and she comes upstairs and she says, "Mommy, Daddy's blue car is not here!" and I said so what does that mean, maybe he's in the garage, go look in the garage, go look around the house, he's in the backyard somewhere, and so she's like, "OK!"'

Gina, who had barely spoken, suddenly interjected, roused by the memory of the end of the ordeal. 'I had the TV so loud but I heard her coming up and down the stairs, I heard Jocelyn whispering and I just sat there, listening to everything, and just kept watching TV.' She fell silent again.

Amanda continued, 'I don't see anything, so I finally tell Jocelyn OK,' and she followed her daughter downstairs, into the forbidden area of the house.

That day she'd been left unchained. Castro was always downstairs when that happened. But he was nowhere to be seen. Amanda took her chance. 'Then I try to open the door, the screen door, and there's like a lock on there, like a chain lock, and so I'm like oh my gosh, and I noticed as I looked at it that you have to have a key to unlock it and open the door and so I'm like pushing it, I'm thinking like, oh it's gonna break easy, it's just a screen door, but it didn't break and so at that point I am yelling and screaming.' The space was just about six inches wide. Enough for her to try to draw attention. 'There was just about that much room that I could fit my arm through and so I have my arm waving, like going crazy, like somebody please help me!'

There was somebody. There was somebody. Two men, Angelo Cordero and Charles Ramsey, saw her, heard her, went to her aid. Ramsey said, 'I see this girl going nuts, trying to get out of this house, so we kick the bottom, and she comes out with a little girl and she says, call 911!' And so they did. 'I've been kidnapped, and I've been missing for ten years, and I'm here, I'm free now!'

Back in the house, Gina sat with the TV on loud. 'I didn't hear her screaming, I just heard when the cops like start to break into the house and stuff. I'm not thinking of the cops, I'm thinking, "Oh no, he found her, and she's gonna be in big trouble."'

The cops involved called dispatch; their words were tinged with elation and disbelief. 'We've found them! We've found them! Yeah, we've got a female conscious and breathing. She's got a young child with her. Make it two. We also have a Michelle Knight in the house!'

Amanda and Jocelyn were free. 'They put me into the back of the car when they went into the house to get Gina and Michelle and then they walked us all to the ambulance, so that was like the first time that we were together and we were like talking freely. And she [Gina], me and her were sitting next to each other and she looks at me and she says, "Wow! Like we are really free?"' Finally, they really were.

The girls were reunited with their families, given medical care, started their long journey back to try to reach that 'normalcy' that Amanda yearned for.

On 6 May 2013, the nightmare that three young women had lived for more than a decade ended. Ariel Castro was arrested within hours.

On 8 May 2013, Castro pleaded guilty to 937 criminal counts of rape, kidnapping and aggravated murder. Before his sentence was handed down, he addressed the court for almost twenty minutes, said he was a 'good person' and 'not a monster' but that he was addicted to sex and porn. He claimed that he had never tortured the women and that 'most' of the sex had been consensual. He asked for their forgiveness with all of the delusion of his previous comments. 'I hope they can find it in their hearts to forgive me because we had a lot of harmony going on in that home.'

The court was unconvinced. He was sentenced to life, plus 1,000 years in prison, without the possibility of parole.

On 3 September 2013, one month into his sentence, Castro hung himself, using bedsheets in his cell. He was fifty-three. He was a brutal and terrible human. He was also Jocelyn's father.

Amanda and Gina now work to help missing children in their situation. I hope that appearing on *Newsnight* played a small part in letting them reclaim their voices and their lives after the trauma they endured. The interview remains one of the most watched in *Newsnight*'s history.

6

Cat and Mouse: Julian Assange

Limp. Clammy. Indifferent. His handshake was like that of a shy teen, forced to abide by social conventions. Retrieving his hand took a little too long, the middle finger lingered on my palm, leaving what felt like a moist trail. I shuddered.

The man himself was a shell. Thin, pale, with sunken eyes. He moved like someone far older. His steps were laboured, his breathing heavy. His cheeks had a kind of grey tinge that I had only seen in prisons. He wasn't getting any sun, wasn't exercising, was barely eating or sleeping.

As he welcomed us into his temporary home – the Ecuadorian Embassy in Knightsbridge – the air was thick, lingering on your clothes, in your nostrils, reeking of despair.

I'd smelt it before, felt that kind of quiet desperation. Years later, Assange would end up in Belmarsh prison – a place reserved mainly for high-profile men who pose a threat to our national security. But this was in Knightsbridge, a stone's throw from Harrods, one of the wealthiest neighbourhoods in the country.

I had visited Belmarsh a few times. The exterior is a generic brown brick, surrounded by high walls, barbed wire, security cameras, barriers and prison vans. Nothing unusual but, unlike other prisons, the sights and smells of Belmarsh would never leave me. It held 900 of the most dangerous criminals this country has seen: Ronnie Biggs, Abu Hamza, Ian Huntley, Tommy Robinson, Charles Bronson.

The Ecuadorian Embassy, however, is a mere ninety-second walk from Knightsbridge tube station. Past Zara, then Harrods. Housed inside a beautiful Edwardian mansion block, just off Basil Street, the red, yellow and blue flag hanging proudly outside. Flats here sell for many millions, Porsches and Bentleys line the streets and Chanel handbags pepper the pavement. Wealth flaunts its presence. For almost seven years, this was Julian Assange's home, although he could only see it from the balcony.

I managed to get an interview with him in 2015, three years into his stay. He'd entered the embassy on 12 June

2012. He had rung the bell, announced himself, walked in and claimed diplomatic asylum. Wanted by the Swedish authorities for questions concerning various allegations of sexual assault, he'd absconded after breaching his bail, fearful he'd be extradited to the United States to face charges of espionage. The Ecuadorian government granted him asylum, sparking a major diplomatic row with the British government. There was a full-blown siege situation. Metropolitan Police officers swarmed outside the stucco gates, ready to arrest him if he ever ventured out.

Few people inspired this combination of passionate admiration, fear, vitriol and disgust. Assange, to many, was the ultimate truth-seeker. He was also a threat to national security, guilty of espionage and possibly rape.

I had always tried to be open minded and impartial about criminal clients and news guests. But this time, it was challenging. Although I'd represented some alleged rapists myself in my previous legal career, I felt a particular discomfort about Assange. The adulation these figures invoke makes people overlook their faults.

That Assange was a celebrity was without question. And he had celebrity pals – Pamela Anderson, a rumoured girlfriend, visited. Noam Chomsky popped by during a London visit; the two men were photographed sharing views and smiles on the balcony. Vivienne Westwood was a regular. The embassy became his private social club.

Initially, he was held there in a secret operation called 'Operation Guest'. It was later renamed 'Operation Hotel'. It was a subtle but telling tweak – the relationship was souring. The embassy wasn't very big and he shared the space with his various lackeys. The rest of the place was the home of the ambassador and his family, and the working home of the staff. Initially, Assange slept in a small, modest room close to that much-photographed balcony. Then, he started to spread. Month by month he took up more space. A back room became a bedroom. His entourage occupied half of the kitchen. Computers and documents spilled over as he claimed more ground.

Letters and gifts arrived for him. Flowers would have to be thrown out immediately, according to the rules laid down by the embassy. Demonstrators pledged their support outside. First in droves, diminishing every year, a rag tag bunch by the end. Assange's mood was congenial for the first year or so but it diminished little by little. By the time we arrived, the atmosphere was very tense.

I was feeling tense too. The interview was a scoop, and I'd been chasing him for ages. But when he finally got back to me, I'd almost declined, because of how tricky it was going to be. Not the logistics, not my personal discomfort, but the content. He was plugging his book, *The WikiLeaks Files: The World According to US Empire*. One of the ways he'd been spending his time was commissioning a series of essays, from academics and experts around the world, about the international impact of WikiLeaks. It wasn't exactly a two-sided account. The contents were, unsurprisingly, supportive of him and his work, with a critical eye on the United States. Six hundred pages of it. The publishers had made it clear to me that he was very keen to direct the conversation about the contents only, while facing rape charges and extradition and hiding from the world. It was a tricky balance. We don't agree terms and conditions, but we accept that sometimes an interviewee has one aim – to plug their works – and we have the opposite – to get a news line and hold them accountable. I was a little uncomfortable with the balance here. We'd been told we had a strict, timed, six minutes only. It would be on a stopwatch. We'd be cut off if we overran. For a man who had endless time on his hands, he was very demanding about not wasting it.

It would be a game of cat and mouse. He would avoid being lured into contentious territory and we would try to get to the heart of his troubles. With someone as clever as Assange, it was a real gamble.

But Ian Katz had decided it was worth the punt. Ian had known him personally – he was one of the *Guardian* journalists who broke the WikiLeaks stories. That pioneering collaboration had ended in distrust and threats of litigation. I hoped this wouldn't be the same.

High-profile interviews were usually conducted by experienced presenters, but it was a last-minute 'get' so the investigation's correspondent, Nick Hopkins, was doing the interview instead. He was a talented and diligent reporter whom Ian had hired from the *Guardian*. But he wasn't a presenter, which meant I was jumpy. The producer who was coming had a father who was a 'fan' and wanted a book signed. That made me even jumpier. I don't have a picture of me with anyone we've interviewed – I don't like to blur the lines. Except one I was forced into, by accusations of being a 'grump' – a team picture after an interview with Emma Thompson. And so we had a producer who wanted her book signed, an interviewer new to TV and a very cagey guest.

The policing of the embassy during the first few years of Assange's stay was said to cost almost £7 million. You could see why. When I arrived, too early, I walked around the block. There were heavy duty armed officers stationed outside. Once I'd been buzzed in, there was a dark and winding staircase. The police presence intensified. I wasn't being allowed in yet. I was to wait in the stairwell. I had my passport ready, formal means of identification. I waited with the officers. A chatty one had experience in high-value diplomatic protection. He'd swapped looking after Presidents and Prime Ministers for guarding the life of a man he barely ever saw. Boring. Of course, he was far too professional to say it.

Finally, I was allowed inside. Well, into the reception. The embassy staff were none too thrilled. I had various documents checked, questions asked – it was like a tiny Assange airport security outfit. Next, I was to be taken to the room we were filming in. I had hoped it would be his bedroom so we'd get a peek inside, but no such luck. The room was far too small for the crew to set up properly, the lighting was dim, and too many people were hanging about. One of Assange's people reminded me of the agreement: six minutes on the clock. I nodded, confident we could push it a little. But then I saw he had a stopwatch and felt much less hopeful.

I asked if Assange slept in this room. They were evasive on any details. I looked around. The walls, once cream, were faded and a little stained. I wondered if this was because of the smoke from his pipe. A shiny wooden table took up about a third of the room. Interviewer and interviewee would have to sit closely to fit in the shot.

The dust danced around us as the extra lighting came on. The rest of the team arrived, making us crammed and claustrophobic.

Nick Hopkins looked twitchy. He was in his late forties, around the same age as Assange, but I couldn't help questioning whether he would be enough of a match. I just hoped he'd find a way to scrutinise him in such limited time.

Finally, the door creaked open and Assange appeared in its frame. Tall, gangly, with long white hair, he had the look of an ageing pop star. His high forehead was speckled with beads of sweat, a neat beard covering the lower half of his face. He wasn't exactly friendly or unfriendly. He didn't smile or scowl. He seemed utterly indifferent, wearied perhaps by the media circus, or the frustrations of his life, or both. He shuffled towards me and shook my hand. I mustered a smile but he didn't bother. His hand in mine made me uneasy.

He exchanged welcomes with the rest of the team and sank into his chair, expelling more dust. His long legs extended well into Nick's little space. They were just inches apart. One of his people gave us the nod, stopwatch in hand. Assange grabbed a copy of the book. We didn't like, or usually allow, a book to be on set like that. But time was too short to do anything about it. I just hoped he wouldn't read from it. That would be one hell of a delaying tactic.

Nick started off asking why he'd felt the book was needed. Assange, glassy eyed, replied slowly. 'Well, that's really interesting, and it's the question I address in the introduction. Why is there a need to do this? Because, in the newspapers, you've heard about WikiLeaks, and in several other publications over a number of years, so what possibly more can the book add? Well, the press, the newspapers and so on tend to just have a very minute focus, sometimes politically biased, but just, you know, it's like swatting little flies. And what we want to under- stand is the general relationships between the United States and other countries, and how other countries work together . . .'

My mind was already wandering as he rambled. We were thirty seconds in. I looked around the crowded room and imagined Pamela Anderson here. I'd seen her in a pantomime once – a haze of curls, lip gloss, red and feathers. Had she been Assange's lover, I wondered. When she had started to visit, it was a paparazzi's dream. Hard to imagine the environment being conducive to romance, let alone private enough.

Assange stopped speaking, barely moving. Nick asked, 'Does this reflect a sense of your frustration that WikiLeaks hasn't been entirely appreciated yet?' Assange stayed still, robotic in tone. 'Well, in the academic sphere something really interesting has happened. So, if you look at papers being published in Spanish, or in Asian languages, or in Slavic languages, there's about thirty thousand references to WikiLeaks. In court papers, in the ECHR [European Court of Human Rights], and in technical papers. But, in the field of foreign relations, there isn't in English, and that's a real mystery, a mystery that I investigate, and solve, in the book...'

More waffle and another mention of the book clasped in his lap. He was determined to plug it in every answer. 'It is in fact direct censorship, admitted by the editors of the most prestigious foreign relations journal *ISQ* because they're worried about the legal risks of citing cables...'

Ninety dull seconds so far. It wouldn't improve unless Nick could get him away from book-related details, away from the Assange-as-hero narrative.

Nick raised the problem of Assange's notoriety. 'But isn't the problem here, the book is a collection of WikiLeaks greatest hits, but if you ask people out in the street about WikiLeaks, they don't think about the 2.3 million cables, they may not read this book. What they think of is *you*!' He raised his voice. He pointed his finger at the impassive Assange for emphasis. They were too close to do that. It looked needlessly aggressive.

Assange exhaled wearily. 'Well, I don't know, I don't know where you get those figures from but actually we did polling in the United States and WikiLeaks name recognition is seven times my name recognition . . . You need a book [mention 3] – foreign relations is a very serious, complex issue, so you need a book [mention 4] length format to tackle it.'

Nick tried again. 'Won't critics say about this book that many of the writers you have, that have written about Russia and Turkey and such like, they all come with an agenda of their own?' Assange didn't look so impassive then. 'Well, they are professors and quite well-regarded journalists with long histories.'

My mind wandered again.

Nick tried harder, bringing in the critics again. 'But isn't it just possible as well that they don't see the conspiracies maybe you see or some of these writers see?' It wasn't going any better. Assange looked even more annoyed. 'Well, this word "conspiracy", I'm not sure why you're using it. It is a word that's used to undermine people. But these are professors of Asian studies and so on. These are serious people and I think this is a serious book [mention 5].'

There were just two minutes to go.

'But wouldn't you have been better to have got people of a more independent disposition to have written about WikiLeaks?' Assange had lost interest. His answers took up more time and were even more banal. He was winning.

Finally, with ninety seconds left, Nick took his chance. 'WikiLeaks, just coming back to that earlier question, don't you worry that this gets in the way of the book, gets in the way of the message, gets in the way of the cut through that you're seeking? This whole business around you, the Ecuadorian Embassy—' He gestured at the room.

For the first time, Assange moved; he raised his voice, interrupted loudly, forcefully. 'Yeah, it does, it does sometimes. It's true. And it is a concern sometimes. On the other hand, sometimes it can be used to draw attention to issues that we want attention drawn to. And sometimes there are overlaps, and the overlaps are fascinating.'

Following Assange quoting extensively from the dreaded book, Nick had a final crack, with only sixty seconds left on the clock. So far, we had nothing newsworthy. 'Mr Assange, would you have done anything differently over the last three years?' 'Sure,' he replied, 'thousands of little things. But, in terms of the big things, it's quite hard to see what difference there could be. It's, it's—'

Nick knew he could miss his chance. He made one last try. It had a hint of defeat. He jumped in loudly, an octave too high. 'Go to America! Face your critics!'

Assange ignored him and continued his final monologue. 'It's interesting, it's a bit like, it's a bit like foreign relations to a degree. You often wonder how much of everything is a forced move, a forced move on politicians, they simply had no other choice. And how much could they simply decide to act in a slightly different manner. Did they make conceptual mistakes, or were there multiple options that they didn't choose? That's a very interesting question that I've dealt with for, I suppose, ten years now. And we see foreign relations specialists dealing with all the time.'

The stopwatch hit six minutes. We were given the signal. The interview came to an abrupt end. 'Mr Assange, thank you.' Assange leant forward in his chair. Gave Nick a handshake again. I could see that it was firmer this time. 'Thank you very much.' The hint of a smile. For good reason.

The cameras stopped rolling. People ushered him out. The producer got her autograph. She was happy. I was not. Assange left as quickly as he'd arrived, closed the door firmly behind him. We'd been in his presence for less than ten minutes.

Despite being this fascinating character, the interview was a dud. We were played and we probably should have known better. It reminded us of our own hubris. We thought we were in control – that he would give us something headline-worthy – but, of course, why would he? And what made us think we could outsmart him?

Eventually, Assange lost all his privileges. No visitors and not even an internet connection. His asylum would be withdrawn on account of 'discourteous and aggressive behaviour'. Lenín Moreno, the new President of Ecuador, said his government had revoked it because of Assange's 'repeated violations to internal conventions and daily-life protocols'.

The WikiLeaks founder was led kicking and screaming from the embassy at about 10.25 a.m. on Thursday 11 April 2019. He'd been there for seven years. He was, by now, entirely dishevelled, thinner and paler than I remembered. He'd long given up on using the balcony – his fear of snipers kept him inside for the final years. As he left, he shouted, 'The UK has no sovereignty!' and 'The UK must resist this attempt by the Trump administration!' But this time it was he who was cut short, as five officers bundled him into a van.

Things moved fast. He appeared before Westminster magistrates a few hours later, found guilty of breaching the terms of his bail. On 1 May 2019, Assange was sentenced to fifty weeks in prison. His new home was HMP Belmarsh. From Knightsbridge to Woolwich.

Sajid Javid, Home Secretary at the time, thanked the Ecuadorian government and the Metropolitan Police. 'No one is above the law,' he concluded. Though Assange had had a pretty good go.

7

Celebrity Culture: Amy Schumer

Whenever I am asked about the worst interview I've ever worked on the answer is not Julian Assange; it was with the American comedian Amy Schumer.

It should have been a highlight of my career. When the new Editor Ian Katz arrived I'd asked him who in the world he'd most like on the programme. If you'd asked me, I'd have gone big: Vladimir Putin, the Pope, Kim Jong Un or Hillary Clinton. Now it'd be Joe Biden, Kamala Harris, President Macron, Angela Merkel, Donald Trump or the Queen. But he said, 'Amy Schumer.' I probably looked a little blank. I mean, I knew who she was. I'd watched some of her sketches. They were vaguely amusing, and she was pretty famous, but I couldn't see the point of an interview. I wasn't senior enough to question his reasons so she became my next goal.

I've long been bemused by the growing interest in celebrities' perspectives and opinions. When I first started working at *Newsnight*, it was mostly an American obsession. Where did Kim Kardashian stand on the death penalty? What does Angelina Jolie think about the situation in the Middle East? But then, celebrities were impacting how average Americans were voting. For a long time, it wasn't very British to care.

The problem is a simple one: if fame precedes the 'issues' – as with so many celebrities whose fame is not issues-based – there's a much higher degree of risk being taken in an intimate interview setting. When that setting is an actual news programme, the risk increases exponentially. In the last decade especially, celebrity has encroached in a very real way on what constitutes 'news' and puts programmes like *Newsnight* in a very awkward position. Do we ignore the rise of celebrity opinion as 'newsworthy'? If we feature more celebrities, are we diminishing what 'news' is even further? It was a constant conundrum.

For my part, I didn't care one jot what they thought about the issues of the day, but I now worked in an environment where their opinions increasingly made headlines. It's a delicate balance. To try to justify having them on a highbrow programme like ours, you'd find yourself coming up with some whizzy current affairs question every time they appeared. What did *Breaking Bad*'s Bryan Cranston think about geopolitics? Where does Naomi Campbell stand on wokeism? What does Susan Sarandon think about the upcoming US elections? How would Eric Cantona be tackling populism in France? It's an ongoing challenge to find something compelling to a *Newsnight* audience. We have to convince the viewer that the celebrity in question is worth their time. To show them where and how the celebrity interacts with news and current affairs. It'd be the producer's job to find something to make it work. Essentially, we'd be looking to escape the criticism that this kind of content was 'dumbing down' – a fair point in my view.

If I was pursuing a celebrity interview, I'd always ask myself what three interesting things they could convincingly speak to that might intrigue a *Newsnight* audience. When we interviewed the Oscar-winning *Black Panther* actress Lupita Nyong'o, we'd had a fascinating conversation with her about global racism, colourism and white supremacy. With the *Peep Show* comedian David Mitchell, we'd asked him to give a three-point plan to improve Britain and its politics. These questions got them over the line into being relevant and the audience loved them both. Online, they became two of the most watched interviews we'd had.

Some celebrities are very smart and extremely influential on issues that matter, especially to younger viewers – the environment, women's rights, racism, homophobia, education, healthcare. But they are rarely at the intellectual forefront of these fields so the debate could be a little staid. Every time you have one on, it's a gamble.

Which type would Amy Schumer be? I wasn't sure. Would most of our audience know who she was? I always felt that if I had to introduce someone extensively, it probably meant they weren't right for the show. Even if they were 'internet famous'. But because I still wanted to stay on the right side of the Editor, I began searching for ways to approach her. I knew she was vocal about body image, and we'd be able to ask about that, and feminism too, and then we could talk about her politics. Generic, but enough to make it work. No doubt, like most of Hollywood, she'd be an avid Democrat, and anti-Republican, an eternal problem for editorial balance whenever someone famous comes on. 'Find me a Republican celebrity!' was an ongoing request. But what else? I just didn't think our viewers would care enough to make the chase worthwhile. But I continued.

142

Over the years, Editors took vastly different positions on whether we should have celebrities on. Each would have a position that they stuck to, and which would affect the show's content and feel. My first Editor, Peter Barron, took the view that if they were globally famous we should have them on and try to make them relevant to our audience. Think Paul McCartney or David Bowie. My last boss, Esme Wren, would only have someone if she felt the news content came before the celebrity status – if we could justify them as being pertinent to social or global affairs. There's justification for Susan Sarandon or Elton John. But Ian Katz loved the cult of celebrity. He embraced it enthusiastically, dismissing the parameters set by earlier Editors. Thanks to him we saw Kirsty Wark dancing to Michael Jackson's 'Thriller' at the end of one programme. He was also in charge when Emily Maitlis got to interview the Cookie Monster from *Sesame Street*. The reception was mixed. Some people thought it was fun and innovative. Others thought it was facile and pointless.

Even though I had asked the question, Ian had tasked my colleague Hannah with getting Schumer on board. She found the agent and sent in her pitch. I didn't get to have any input. It was declined immediately. I suspected I'd have had a better chance if I'd done it myself. But now that opportunity was gone.

Then, months later, Schumer's team announced a book, her first memoir. The material would focus on all of the body image and the feminist issues we'd wanted to discuss. Here was a new opportunity.

Of course, I was desperate to negotiate this to impress the boss. And I could tell the publicist straightforwardly that Schumer was the Editor's 'dream interview' and leave it at that. She invited me into her office to discuss our pitch. I prepared meticulously.

The pitch was simple – Maitlis meets Schumer. Emily was doing a lot more programmes by this stage. She was effectively the second presenter to Evan Davis. She'd left being a sporadic host behind and was being lined up for more and more shifts. Most UK publicists wanted their clients to be interviewed by her, as she was high profile, glamorous, professional and, crucially, she always read the book in advance and prepared thoroughly. And so, she had star power in the UK, but Schumer would never have heard of her. Barely any US guests had. So, we'd have to offer more. I said we'd do a wide-ranging interview covering all of the topics in the memoir. We'd make sure it ran at length, maybe six or seven minutes, we'd plug it all over our social media channels, we'd get Emily to do an article about the whole experience. These were the only stops I could pull out. I just hoped that it would work.

Months later, we finally got Ian Katz his prize – Schumer's team agreed to let us have her first UK interview. There was one problem – the date they'd offered was actually Emily's birthday. But she knew it mattered to Ian and agreed to do it anyway. We both hoped to score brownie points.

So far, so good. The book arrived, Emily read it all, the brief got prepped. We'd mix in the political questions, add a dash of *Newsnight* highbrow to mingle with the more popular content. It seemed an easy hit.

We'd arranged to do the filming at Schumer's hotel in Holborn. She wasn't going to come into the studio. That was the norm when recording interviews with celebrities or world leaders. Either because they had too many pressures on their time, for security or, with some, maybe they felt they were too important to make a trip. Many of them didn't like doing an interview live either – they thought they had more control if it was pre-recorded. It gave them a chance to demand things be changed or dropped (not that we ever agreed to that, unless there was some legal issue). It allowed them to redo an answer if they lost their train of thought, or felt they missed a point. For us? Organising a pre-record took up a lot more time: it's more expensive, it involves a lot of camera crew and travel and, most challenging of all, it means we need to organise a room to do the interview in.

I spent a lot of time arranging venues. You'd think that they'd be conducted on site, in the huge BBC building, new Broadcasting House, that looms just north of Oxford Circus. But no. There are basically no rooms that can accommodate a high-quality TV interview shoot. There's only one – called the 'Council Chamber' – that is large enough, nice enough, quiet enough, to allow for the sprawling needs of TV cameras and lighting. The rest? Tiny meeting rooms or open-plan areas. Not a single other room that can be used for a pre-recorded interview. It's an absurd problem. We don't even have access to a full-time studio. Access starts late in the evening, way after we record interviews in the day. You'd have to get special permission to get the studio crew to do anything even thirty minutes earlier. Basically, beg for them to help us out. Often it wasn't possible. So, the hunt for rooms was eternal.

A guest's representative would ask, 'Where do we come to?' assuming they'd be hosted and recorded in some slick TV studio. Then we'd scramble to find, and pay for, a separate external room or suite or venue. Or ask them to accommodate us – many of the embassies knew the issue so would kindly offer their own rooms if one of their leaders or ministers agreed to talk to us. So, you'd record an interview with Justin Trudeau at the

Canadian High Commission in Trafalgar Square. A conversation with President Netanyahu, with two hours of security checks, in his hotel suite. A chat with the French Foreign Minister at the ambassador's residence in Notting Hill. For other guests, I was always very worried about spending licence fee payers' money. I'd walk to venues when possible. Take the bus if not. It was a stark difference between many producers and people higher up the BBC hierarchy. It's not that every presenter or executive didn't think about this, but they'd become used to taxis and nice hotels. Every year, the BBC would publish the expenses for many of the top executives. We'd find it impossible to resist looking, gasping at some of the more outrageous figures. We'd be as irritated as, no doubt, many of the members of the public would feel seeing some of the money being spent. My personal bugbear shall remain nameless. The sometime presenter, whose job seems vague and overpaid, once claimed more money in taxi expenses than I earned in an entire year. Actually, not once, several times. I'd check to see if I'd finally managed to out-earn his taxi expenses every year. I never did.

It infuriated me for several reasons. First, it gave the impression that everyone at the Corporation was extravagant (not true) and compounded the view that some executives were overpaid and thoughtless about how their behaviour impacted on the rest of us (often true). The chasm between that tier of the organisation – in terms of pay and workload – and the rest of us grated on many.

One of the worst things was the nomenclature. Producers were known as 'production' or 'editorial'. The presenters? They'd be called 'the talent'. It's a curiously divisive categorisation. As if, somehow, we were all the 'untalented'.

The UK book publicist was one of the best in the business. She never let us down. She got the books to us early and never made any demands on questions or content. She knew exactly what she was doing. She was easy to deal with and loyal to the programme. When I arrived, the hotel room allocated was ideal. They'd generously let us have it at a discount and it looked glamorous.

All seemed fine. Nothing was awry. Amy's agent arrived – Amy was on her way. Emily came too. Everything was in place.

But you can't account for everything. Amy was in the hotel, we were told, but just wanted to see her boyfriend first. She might be slightly late. Lateness makes everything more stressful. We have tight schedules, edits to do and it was going to eat even more into Emily's birthday.

With little fanfare, Amy eventually appeared.

There's a moment when the guest arrives when you can tell if it's going to work or not. If there's going to be a rapport. If the celebrity is in a good or bad mood. If they want to be there. If they are tired, jetlagged or annoyed. If they're bored. In the first seconds that Amy arrived, I knew we were in trouble.

She looked tired and uncomfortable. Perhaps she was. From her point of view, it can't be much fun traipsing around the world, being dragged into dark rooms, having to bare your soul over and over again. With a news interview like this, it wasn't just us taking a gamble, she was taking one too. She was exposing herself to the risk of being asked about all kinds of things she may have no interest in, or expertise in. I only hoped she'd warm up.

As I watched the two women in their respective chairs being set up with their microphones, I reflected on the particular issues that came with dealing with conversations of this kind. With a politician or a global leader, an economist or a philosopher, you have a certain understanding of how they're likely to behave. Things may get fiery, but it's basically a predictable pattern, an intellectual game of cat and mouse. With a celebrity, it's often much more personal and thereby unpredictable. There can be demands galore, random answers, incoherent narratives, petulance and ennui. It's another reason I was less keen on negotiating with them. One time, a famous male star requested $2,000 for his hair and make-up. I suggested he splashed his face in the loo and combed his hair for free. Miraculously, we still got that one! Another time I was shouted at so loudly by a celeb's representative that the whole office gathered to watch. I had no interest in meeting the 'famous'. Give me an afternoon with a Foreign Minister over a female comedian any day.

Emily was doing her very best to thaw the atmosphere – working overtime to be congenial before recording began. We exchanged a glance. We both knew this wasn't going to be easy.

Unlike with Assange, it was the presenter who held the book. The book was there to show that she'd read it. To reassure the celebrity that it wasn't going to be all news and current affairs questions. That we'd done our job to digest their content. Emily held it firmly, scanning her questions on a small piece of paper which she held against the book.

As we started to record, I opened my notebook. One of the producer's jobs is to work out, as the interview is recorded, what bits are the best. I used my notes as a memory aid once the cameras were switched off, putting stars next to parts I thought were news lines, using highlighters to mark up sections I wanted to keep – yellow for definite keeper, pink for parts I'd decide in the edit. It'd be left blank if it wasn't going to make the cut. We'd get about twenty-five minutes with Amy. We'd probably use about six minutes. It's a lot to cut out. About 75% would need to go. Something always goes wrong. You have to get the material into a machine that looks like it's from 1970 (the BBC always feels a decade behind most of the other broadcasters for up-to-date methods and cutting-edge technology). Then you'd get it digitally transferred into the editing room. Wait for an editor to arrive to help you. Go through it over and over, honing and perfecting your content to the best six minutes you could find. Often the system would crash. You'd need a restart. Maybe some of the edit was lost. You'd have to start again. Beg the programme Editor for a bit more time to make fewer cuts. Then, the editor would go for a meal break. Maybe the edit wouldn't make sense when you played it back. You'd need to reorder some parts to make it cohere. It was always a race against time. The minutes would pass so fast, sometimes you'd even still be doing it just before the programme aired. I'd never mastered being calm while doing it. I'd feel the tick tock of the clock during the whole process.

So, I sat poised, ready to take down the content in note form.

Emily began with a soft question, which I hoped would improve the atmosphere. 'The bit in your book that really struck a chord with me, and I haven't heard anyone describe it, I don't think, was the introversion – that women constantly feel it's up to them to fill the gaps and smooth over the social awkwardness and just provide the chatter, and I'm wondering about the moment when you suddenly went, oh I don't have to?'

The question was ironic in the circumstances. Schumer looked reticent and Emily was likely to need to fill the gaps *and* smooth over the social awkwardness herself. I hoped for the best, and got ready to transcribe the response.

Schumer began: 'Probably sooner than I should have, but it was, yeah, going to a wedding with my boyfriend at the time and I just was in like in my mid-twenties and was just like I really hate this. And, um, I can't do it, I can't be this social with this many people for this long. And errr, and getting to a place where I didn't think something was wrong with me, and that I thought it was OK and I really like that I know that I need time on my own to recharge.'

She stopped. The answer was peppered with pauses and wouldn't make the cut. I left it blank. I hoped she'd improve.

Emily tried again. 'And do you say "no" to more weddings now, I mean are there just events where you say

"I cannot stand that, I cannot be there"?' The questions were so far removed from Emily's daily content. They didn't sit well with me, or with her. Schumer gave her second response. 'Yeah, or I can just go for the bare minimum. I can't do a weekend, a full weekend wedding. I mean, errr, and you know my friends are still getting married, we are like thirty-five, can we stop, like why are people still doing this? But it's more than that. It's not just affairs that are that big. It can be just the small talk with someone in the elevator . . .'

The conversation was banal. I transcribed it. But a lot of it would need to be edited out. I wish I could tell you that things improved, that the answers began to be more coherent, more interesting, as the interview progressed, but it just wasn't the case. I kept waiting for something I could highlight even just in pink. Eventually, I realised it just wasn't coming. There's a sinking disappointment when that happens. All that work, all that hope, and you leave with something that you know is subpar. I just held on, hoping that Schumer would say something thought-provoking, or news making, when we got to the political part.

By now it was September 2016. The race for the White House was on. Hillary Clinton versus Donald Trump. There were two months to go. Clinton's side painted her as a brilliant and experienced leader, an internationalist, a great orator, a compassionate feminist, the best woman to be the USA's first female President. Her enemies saw her as a Washington insider, an elitist who only had her profile because of her husband, and who would do nothing to protect the ordinary person and shake up the status quo. On the other side, Donald Trump. A wealthy reality TV star and successful populist, who wanted to 'Make America Great Again'. I was absolutely certain Trump was going to win.

Schumer had been talking about her fears and issues for quite some time now. I'd mostly zoned out, just transcribing and waiting for something I could use. We'd done introversion. Weddings. Body image. What it's like being famous. We'd done about fifteen minutes. I knew politics was next.

'You say the name Hillary Clinton in America, you'll get incredible responses,' Emily said. 'There'll be those who love her and there'll be those with visceral hatred for her.'

I awaited Schumer's response. Pen poised. She looked a little irritated. 'Well, that's what I am saying with them not being informed, because those people aren't informed. You know, if you go, "Why don't you like Hillary?" they'll go, "She lied about her emails! What else is she gonna lie about?" People get one fact and that's what they latch on to about a candidate. You know, they go she lied about that and I'll go, "Well, Donald Trump has a fake college! Donald Trump doesn't pay his workers. He won't release his taxes. There's never been a nominee who's ever not released their taxes," sooooo, um, I don't think you can. Umm, I haven't had a conversation with anyone who doesn't like Hillary where they've had anything meaning-ful to say!' She appeared annoyed. Her response was clas-sic celebrity – pro-Democrat, dismissive, generic. But at least it was on a topic that the viewer would care about. The transcript had its first use of the yellow highlighter. I felt a modicum of relief.

Emily tried for more. 'If it isn't Hillary in November, does your act change? Does your outlook change?' Schumer shook her head. It was unclear what her mood was now; she just looked distracted. 'My act will change because I will need to learn to speak Spanish. Cos I will move to Spain. Or somewhere. It's beyond my compre-hension if Trump won! It's just . . . It's toooo crazy.'

The yellow highlighter came out: 'Amy Schumer says she will move to Spain if Trump wins.' We had enough to justify having done it. Just. Over twenty minutes in.

I hoped we'd get a bit more in this vein. But time was drawing to a close, and Schumer was famous for one more thing. For sex. Well, for her depictions of it on screen. It was our last topic.

'Talk to me a little bit about sex,' Emily said. Her hand rested nervously at her throat; she looked uncomfortable. 'The Hollywood portrayals of sex are very squeaky clean, and romantic, and the Amy Schumer portrayal of sex is half the time it's quite crap, you know? You can be quite lazy in bed, nothing much happens, you know, it's . . . it's . . .' Emily trailed off. When she's awkward, she moves her hands around a lot, and they were moving around every time she asked more about sex.

Like most of the presenters and correspondents, sex was not a topic Emily had to mention very often (yet), and it was also one that most of them didn't like to deal with. I could hardly remember any incidences where the topic arose, so to speak, in our daily churn of politics, economics and foreign affairs. But, when it did, I didn't share their discomfort.

Neither did Paul Mason. We'd once worked together on the first broadcast interview with E.L. James – the mega-successful author of *Fifty Shades of Grey*. She wasn't the usual *Newsnight* guest but the book changed how women read, and maybe even what they wanted more generally, so we decided she qualified as a 'zeitgeist' moment. Once she agreed to do it, I started to read the book for the briefing. Paul was presenting that day, and the briefing was very different from our usual ones. I probably deserve an award for keeping a straight face while Paul earnestly enquired about the terms he wasn't sure of, and probably, wisely, was loath to google on a work computer. 'Sam, what's fisting?' is a question I didn't expect during my career. Once I'd told him (please google if you're unsure, *not* on a work computer) he seemed very impressed by my knowledge. And then he was unable to stop saying it. Hence, I have the dubious pleasure of being the person who managed to get the word 'fisting' said not once, but three times on *Newsnight*. It's one of my lesser achievements.

Amy Schumer also seemed strangely circumspect on the topic. Maybe it was because of the froideur in the room, maybe she was tired of talking about it, maybe she'd been asked so many times before, but she could barely muster any enthusiasm in her reply. 'I mean, yeah-hhhh,' she tossed her hair, 'I mean, I don't know the kind of sex you're having . . .' (Emily smiled serenely, her face frozen in a vague look of horror) 'but I am showing the kind of sex that I have mostly had. Usually, if it's not, like, sex within a relationship and you're sleeping with someone new, most likely it doesn't go well, and something weird or hurtful happens.'

Poor Emily. We'd had her come here, on her birthday, to do an interview that was not really working, and now she had to talk about sex. And masturbation. 'Because you're quite graphic. In that, you know, you say this is not a self-help book, but then, it's a sort of "how to" book. It's to show women how to masturbate.'

I looked at the ground. I don't know how she managed to continue. It's a real skill not to show emotion in moments of hilarity and horror. Emily is fantastic at it. I'm not so good. Also, when I'm really amused or tense my whole upper chest flushes bright red and my throat, charmingly, starts to make a kind of burpy noise. I've had to learn to control it to avoid it being heard and distracting people. But I was now in full flush/burp mode. I set my eyes firmly on the carpet while Amy answered, just willing this entire interview to be over.

Her final response summed the whole thing up. It was awkward, and not exactly *Newsnight*'s usual fare. 'Yeah, well, you're right. That's nice. I wish somebody had told me! I had to figure it out on my own when I was like old . . . Like sixteen. I mean that's old. Guys are like jerking off when they're nine . . .' We were coming to the end of the interview. The best part was her ten-second answer about moving to Spain. The rest? Awkward, stilted, bad sex, masturbation and now a reference to nine-year-old boys jerking off. It was really not what we had hoped for. If it hadn't been decreed from on high, perhaps it wouldn't have run at all.

The interview ended. Amy left in that way that only happens when things have gone wrong. Her microphone was discarded first, she jumped up, bolted off to see her boyfriend, and left the rest of us behind, deflated. Emily and I exchanged glances. She let out an almighty puff of air that summed it all up. We never ever had a drink after an interview but that day we did. We both chugged a very large gin martini in seconds. We commiserated over the lack of good content, and then Emily left to enjoy the rest of her birthday as I trawled, slightly tipsy, back to the office to face the edit.

The gamble hadn't paid off for us. I was certain Amy Schumer would say the same.

'How did it go?' Ian asked. I mustered some enthusiasm. I did my best to make it sound good, and cut the content as quickly as possible so I didn't have to think about it again.

If Schumer didn't immediately regret doing the interview, she must have after Tump was elected. The clip about her moving to Spain took on a little life of its own, and she was asked about it repeatedly. When was she leaving? Why had she said it if she wasn't? She mentioned her annoyance in an interview with *Grazia* years later – complaining that we'd asked her a stupid question. It wasn't good journalism and it really illustrated a problem to me: we *probably* shouldn't have had her on and she *probably* shouldn't have been put in a position where she was asked to comment on this in the first place.

By the time Trump took over as President, Ian Katz had announced he was leaving for Channel 4. When he told us he was going, I cried again. This time from relief. I only hoped the next Editor would support me more. I wasn't sure I could handle it if not.

8

The Trump Years – Fake News and Impartiality Woes: Comey, Spicer and Daniels

US President Donald Trump was inaugurated in January 2017 and everything changed. Personal politics aside, his time in office was an absolute boon for news, for journalism and for us at *Newsnight*. His sheer unpredictability left seasoned journalists hanging on his every tweet – we found out about hirings and firings in random missives in the middle of the night. We established what his next policies would be via social media and we waited for the next scandal, blunder or disaster with bated breath. Viewing figures for news programmes soared, people were confused and gripped. It fell to programmes like ours to try to make sense of it all. We were expected to guide people in the new world order. His chaos gave us a chance to provide stability and cool-headed analysis in unprecedented ways. We could establish no pattern to his behaviour. All of the usual apparatus was gone. It was discombobulating and, in news terms, exhilarating.

President Trump considered the press his enemy. Almost all of us, bar a few favourites at Fox News, were considered impediments to his brand and mission. The administration coined some, frankly, inspired phrases to diminish the power of the press. Where there had once been the truth or lies, we now had new areas of under-standing – 'alternate facts' as Kellyanne Conway, Trump's campaign manager and presidential counsellor, phrased it. And the battle between his staff and the press corps in Washington created unforgettable headlines daily. On the one side a President who saw himself as beyond scrutiny, and on the other side, a group of journalists befuddled by his behaviour and trying to hold to account someone who refused to play ball.

'Fake news' was the most brilliant, simple, and deadly, weapon in Trump's arsenal. It created a new dynamic; not one where conversations could be had in good faith, not one where journalists would test and challenge power and policy, not one where it was assumed that debate was a basic tool of freedom of the press and democracy.

Instead, we were liars, peddlers of propaganda. The battle was between the truth and the President, but he framed it as an ideological battle of his patriotism against the destructive machinations of a press that he painted as unwilling to give him fair coverage. The media, so he stated, was inherently 'anti-Trump' and, by implication, against the American people.

He called out journalists and outlets as 'fake news' almost daily. And it became incredibly difficult to deconstruct. At first, it was a strange idea, but very quickly it took hold. So challenging to the old rules about public discourse and to journalism as we knew it.

While America adjusted to its new leader, we were waiting for ours. Now that Ian Katz had left, the process of finding a new Editor had begun. Recruitment in the BBC is, in my experience, completely opaque. You're told nothing. You know nothing. All around you, you have to read countless columns in the *Guardian* or *The Times*, speculating about who is next in line. Betting companies (it's niche, but it happens) compile odds on who the runners and riders are. But us? The actual producers? We know nothing.

Viewing figures had been going down when Katz left but, with Brexit and Trump on the table, it was a golden opportunity for the right person to turn things around and, hopefully, restore *Newsnight* to its former glory. I was hoping it would be someone who loved the interview content and who loathed the gimmicks. Hello to discussions with Presidents. Goodbye to trying to interview *Sesame Street* characters.

Eventually, we were told who the new Editor would be. Esme Wren, who'd been running politics at Sky News. I was delighted for two reasons. First, I'd never had a female Editor and it felt like an important moment. Secondly, I knew a lot of people who had worked with her and heard nothing but great things. Variously, they said she was clever, patient, fair, full of ideas and hard-working.

While we awaited her arrival, Trump made his mark. His world order was populist, protectionist, isolationist and, depending upon your view, either patriotic or nationalistic. He careened into new areas of controversy every day. Ones with real and palpable effects. A travel ban on citizens from several Muslim-majority countries incensed millions and reassured millions more. His plans to 'build a wall' on the border with Mexico caused protests and shock alongside delight from his supporters. His policy on family separations for apprehended migrants appalled many. He left images on the world's consciousness of children in segregated enclosures, 'Kids in cages' as the headlines ran. Many of his comments and actions were seen as racially charged or outright racist, misogynistic or sexist. The press speculated on his health, his wealth, his sanity, his hair, his sex life. Now, nothing was off-limits.

His time in office posed a serious challenge to impartiality. The BBC's great strength is its provision of unbiased and fair content that allows viewers to draw their own conclusions, and not be guided by the supposed or actual biases of the correspondents and presenters they watch. But, with Trump, you could feel the struggle for certain presenters and correspondents to stifle their bias. Their Twitter feeds became more and more close to the mark. Sometimes, they crossed the line. I regret witnessing the BBC's impartiality diminish. You may disagree. But, when I arrived, 'impartiality' was a source of pride to us all. It was our version of the Hippocratic Oath. I cared about it passionately and did all I could to keep my own views and opinions away from my workplace. When I started, I didn't know much, if anything at all, about the political affiliations of my colleagues. It was a genuine surprise to me when Robbie Gibb (my first Deputy Editor) went to work for the Conservative Party. I had never googled him while we worked together and he kept his views to himself. We managed to keep politics out of the office.

As time went on, that discipline palpably receded. The first real blow was Brexit. I remember coming into the office the day after the result came in and one (Remainer) colleague was weeping in the newsroom. I was embarrassed for her. Had I been the Editor, I would have asked her to gather herself and come back when she could show a professional demeanour. But it was the tip of the iceberg. The (small) number of colleagues who were likely (I never asked) Leavers kept a very low profile. It was clear that their view was the minority. The whole building felt like it was in mourning for a while. I wasn't. I was interested in us seeing what happened next, and in reporting on it. I didn't reveal how I had voted, while endless conversations occurred on the topic, and I felt more and more out of kilter with those who felt that the workplace was a venue for their own politics in a way that I did not. It was our job to deliver content, not to shape it with our personal prejudices. That view felt increasingly a minority one and I felt forced to air 'opinions' when I never would have before, to provide counterbalance or challenge 'groupthink'.

With Trump it was acute. People could barely hide their contempt for the man. His view of the liberal media despising and vilifying him was borne out in some of my interactions. After I said that many of his supporters may well be happy with his policies, a self-evident observation, one colleague named me 'the Kellyanne Conway of the office'. I started to feel that it was hard to see my workplace as one that maintained rigorous standards or trusted its viewers to make up their own minds.

Of course, I tried to persuade President Trump to be interviewed. Emily Maitlis had interviewed him several times before and the encounter would have been electric. I made countless requests both officially, through the White House and the US Embassy, and unofficially, through people I knew he knew and contacts I had who had worked for him over the years. Nothing came to fruition. Although we weren't going to get an interview with him – that gift fell to Piers Morgan in the end – I knew there were lots of other interviews that would grip and enthral our audience and hopefully impress the new Editor, when she arrived.

The Trump years created a huge number of new protagonists for a news booker. The ones I'd have loved to have spoken to the most were Kellyanne Conway and Vice President Mike Pence. I knew that was never going to happen. In fact, we never managed to get a single person from the administration. But there were three – James Comey, Sean Spicer and Stormy Daniels – that I had my sights on. I just hoped I could score them all – and I did.

James Comey – April 2018

James Comey, the former Director of the FBI, had accidentally become the biggest story in town. His decision, before the election, to announce the FBI investigation into Hillary Clinton – and those infamous emails – led many to believe he handed Trump the election. An investigation was opened, then closed, then opened again (when even more emails emerged on the laptop of Democrat Congressman Anthony Weiner) and then closed once more, barely hours before the election began. He found himself at the centre of an election scandal. His reward? Trump fired him barely six months later. He found out in a very Trumpian way, when breaking news of his sacking flashed onto the television screen behind him as he was addressing a room of FBI agents in LA. He found out on a stage and reportedly laughed, thinking it was a prank.

James Comey had the air of a lifetime spent in service. He was tall, discreet and self-possessed. He reeked of establishment and quiet power. After his dismissal he kept a composed silence . . . and then he announced his memoirs. It was going to be an interview and a half and I had to have it. The second the book was announced I tracked down the US publisher. The US market barely cares about a UK interview – even if it's for an international broadcaster – and US audiences haven't heard of any of our presenters. So, you usually have to work hard to find out if there's going to be a UK release and, crucially, if there will be a UK interview. The person in question may do tens or dozens of US interviews on their tour. They will probably only do one for the UK market. The odds are therefore stacked against you. I found the UK contact fast, a PR with a great record in delivering content, and then started to lobby him for that one golden opportunity. I knew how much getting it would mean. And I knew how it would look to the new boss too.

A year later, in her book *Airhead: The Imperfect Art of Making News*, Emily Maitlis described lobbying as 'a certain amount of indecent begging'. I'd describe it as a deluge of polite requests, spread over many months, as I tried to sense what could tip the balance in our favour. We had to find Comey's sweet spot – a reason he'd choose us above all others. I knew the *Today* programme on Radio 4 were our main rivals; they'd thrown everything at the interview too. We all had the same offer – a long interview, for an outlet he wouldn't have heard of, with a presenter he wouldn't be aware of, in person. The only

extra lever we had was that we could do a full TV extrava-
ganza and that Emily was such a specialist in the story,
and such an enthusiast, that I knew she could add a lot of
extra value in the kind of minutiae of the story that a brain
like his would enjoy. And so I plugged away, sending new
content we had done that reflected our forensic and fair
approach, calling and emailing the (very patient) PR,
sending over answers to all the many questions Comey's
people had and, crucially, checking in as to what we
needed to adjust or change to win the game. As bad luck
would have it, things got really close when I was on leave,
taking the calls in a rainy park, watching my son career
across a football pitch, boys shouting in the background.
Months and months came down to this moment. And
finally we had it. The exclusive was ours.

Emily, now the new main presenter, and Esme, the
newly arrived Editor, were thrilled. Crucially, I had
managed to negotiate an interview that wasn't coming
after all the US ones. It would be early on in the US schedule. It meant any news lines we got would have far more
impact. It made it more exciting and more pressure for
Emily. We were going to dedicate most of the programme
to it. Twenty-five whole minutes. The longest interview I'd
ever seen on the programme. Emily readied herself and
the book arrived (with the usual NDA). She was so excited

about its content, about what it told her of the story she had been following for so many years, and of the President whom she'd met so many times, that I think she read the book *three* times. Her enthusiasm was contagious. The team worked hard to make a good brief, to get it perfect, and off they flew, Emily and producer Rhoda Buchanan, to New York, to meet the man face to face and take down his testimony on that crucial detail in American history.

On the flight over, Emily read the book once again. She knew the value of the prize and the interview answers were a responsibility. What was the President like? What had he asked of Comey? How had they interacted? When was the animosity apparent? As ever, there's a tension between the fine details of a story – which many of my colleagues care about deeply – and the wider, more 'populist' things that I really enjoyed hearing. Those latter answers often last far longer. They have a shelf life that might never end – and so I wanted to know what Trump's face looked like when his FBI Director told him about allegations that he'd cavorted with Russian prostitutes. I longed to hear how Comey had uttered the words 'golden shower' to the forty-fifth President of the United States. How he'd responded to their very different visions of what the FBI should and could do. I hoped we'd get to hear all about that.

Both of the Deputy Editors were involved in the briefing. There's huge interest in US politics on the team.
Everyone was fired up. There was an added element – the
long interview was due to be done at 11 a.m. US time, 4
p.m. in the UK, and then cut in the afternoon, to broadcast in full that evening. It would be a tense day for Emily.
But, by 10.30 p.m. Emily sat, composure personified, in
our hastily booked Times Square studio. Waiting to see
how it had gone was news torture.

It was strange to finally see the man at the centre of
it all. He looked so calm and collected. I'd read his
book and it was in a similar vein. Almost too calm. I
didn't think I learned that much about him, the man,
but a lot about the details of his job and professional
life. His book was as methodical as you'd imagine the
brain of an FBI Director needed to be. Emily's enthusiasm was writ large in her body language. She looked
engaged and fascinated by his replies. To an average
person in the UK his name probably didn't mean that
much but to a *Newsnight* viewer or US politics obsessive, it meant a lot.

Donald Trump had called Comey a slimeball. He sat
rigidly, upright, military-like, on the sparse chair. His
attire more casual than I expected. Perhaps he'd tired of
the FBI look. His blue suit wasn't quite the perfect fit and

his purple checked shirt was opened a button or two. No tie. As informal as these kinds of interviews get.

Watching the interview back now, so much of it feels safe. At the time, it was revelatory. Perhaps I have become tired of the details of Russian interference and the Mueller report, but, at that moment, it was crucial to Trump's presidency. Emily meticulously took him through every detail – had he messed up in his announcements? Answer: no. Was Putin influencing the election? Probably. Had he politicised the FBI? Absolutely not. Was he guilty of bias, of double standards? Never. Their parry – of two super-well-informed people – went on. I waited for the two things I wanted to know: what did it feel like being sacked in the way that he had been? And how did Trump react when confronted with allegations about his sex life?

I could see my colleagues were enraptured by the political discussion, and I was glad to have given Emily this important interview. I wondered how many viewers felt gripped in the same way. Our audience research usually reveals that the interest the team has in US politics isn't shared as much by the audience but, during Trump's time in office, people had become extremely keen. Was this interview providing them with the same gleeful satisfaction in answering the kinds of questions they'd also mused? Or were they more like me, and keen to know the less salubrious details?

Emily continued; we were now about halfway through . . . my ears pricked up.

'Let's fast forward to January 2017. Trump has won, you're on your way to Trump Tower to tell the President-Elect about a secret dossier – the Steele dossier – allegations of misconduct, conspiracy between Trump's campaign team and the Russian government. Did he seem worried by that?'

Comey responded in a measured way, but his tone belied his low-key contempt, even if he was far too classy to openly articulate it. 'He seemed focused on it in one respect which is to try to confirm that it had no impact on the actual vote.' Emily went on, 'And did that strike you as odd?' Comey nodded. 'Yes, I mean that's a legitimate question for a candidate to ask. What struck me was what wasn't asked, which was so what's next and how do we protect the American democracy from this Russian threat? I don't remember any questions about that.'

Now, we got to the part I had waited for. 'One part of the dossier contains salacious allegations that he ordered prostitutes in a Moscow hotel room to urinate on each other as he watched in a bed that the Obamas had once slept in. You held back from telling him that line. Why?'

Comey looked awkward, no doubt how he had felt that day. 'Because it's hard enough to talk to the President-Elect and use the words "prostitutes" and "Moscow hotel room" in the same sentence, and my goal was to do as little as I needed to do to put him on notice that this was out there. It wasn't something that the FBI was interested in except that we wanted the candidate, now the President-Elect, to know that this was out there. In the event there was something to it, it disarms any effort to coerce an official, but also just because the US intelligence community had this information, and we knew it was going to become public and we wanted him to know.'

He looked ill at ease. Emily pressed him further. 'So it wasn't embarrassment on your part?' Comey was clearly embarrassed, but he replied, 'Discomfort. The whole thing created an out-of-body experience for me. But just discomfort, what am I doing as the FBI Director talking about something like this with the future President, and so I thought I will do my best to discharge my duty to put him on notice, but I don't really want to talk about the rest of that . . .'

We make it to the part where the men spent time alone. Emily went on, 'On several occasions President Trump met with you alone. We heard about the chicken pasta dinner. He demanded your loyalty. Why didn't you just tell him that was not your job?' Comey demurred, 'That's a fair question. I think I kinda did, by first of all staring and not giving a response and then, in the rest of the conversation, interjecting, trying to explain why it's important for there to be distance between the FBI and the Justice Department.'

Trump was obsessed with loyalty. He'd met Comey alone, several times, demanding Comey basically pledge his allegiance to him personally. It was at odds with the very purpose of high-ranking public officials, let alone the Director of the FBI. Comey must have been shocked. 'Well, I think, from what I said, he fairly understood how I thought about my job by both my reactions when he asked for loyalty and what I said during the meal. In hindsight I think it's fair, I might have done it differently, but I don't want to be too tough on myself because I think a fair-minded President would understand the FBI Director just told you in substance, this is not something you should be doing.'

'Did you feel intimidated by him?' Emily persisted. 'Not intimidated by him personally,' Comey replied, though I felt he wasn't telling the truth on that. 'I have tremendous respect for the American presidency, the White House obviously is a central physical place in the life of my country and so the environment is intimidating.

Intimidating is probably the wrong word. It just brings a sense of respect, almost of reverence, into play but I don't think that was a heavy layover for our conversation.'

Emily gave it one more try, to get him to admit he was angry or appalled by this call for 'loyalty'. 'Alarm bells presumably are ringing at this stage. He's demanding loyalty, he wants you on your own, he reminds you, you say, of a mafia boss. Why don't you think I can't do my job, did you think of walking?' Comey shook his head. 'No, actually I thought the opposite – that I can't possibly leave the FBI now, that I need to stay and try to protect its independence.'

And so there it was, a battle between a President insisting on loyalty, and an FBI Director insisting upon independence. It was only ever going to end one way. Trump had fired him, with disregard, and this was his chance to bite back.

'You talk of President Trump staining those around him, what did you mean by that?' Emily asked. Comey was in his stride. 'I think the way in which he acts, especially his corrosive effect on norms, truth telling being the most important of them, has that staining effect on institutions and people who are close to him. He has a habit of, and even people who support him would agree with this I think, of telling lies, sometimes big, sometimes casual, and insisting that the people around him repeat them and believe them. And that is, that stains any human.'

Emily didn't ask him how he felt in that moment, in front of those FBI colleagues, as his career flashed before him, but his calm anger filtered into his responses. 'I wake up some mornings and read the President is demanding the jailing of private citizens, occasionally me, and so that's one of the reasons I am confident the answer is there are not adequate people around him to stop impulsive behaviour. And we've actually become numb to it in the United States. Our President calling for the imprison-ment of private citizens. That is not OK, that is not normal in the United States of America. Or in the UK. It's not acceptable and so that is an attack on some of the norms that are at the core of this country and we cannot allow ourselves to become numb to that.'

It was a familiar narrative – Trump is inept, Comey is upstanding. Nothing is that simple. Luckily, Emily had a question that could capture some nuance. 'If you step back, you say look at Trump, his poll ratings are up, his taxes are down, he's planning on a second term, he's got credible Western allies supporting his foreign policy deci-sions, he's pulled off this extraordinary coup of a meeting with North Korea. Plenty of people are saying, things aren't going so badly.'

Comey responded measuredly – and evasively. 'Look, I want the President to succeed. I want every US President to succeed. If he's able to achieve a resolution in North Korea, that is a great thing for the country and the world, that'd be wonderful. I continue to have the concern I have about his effect on our core values, and so despite that I hope there's lots of successes in the rest of the Trump administration. That doesn't mean we shouldn't focus on the threat that his conduct poses to what matters most in this country, which is our values.'

That was it. It was over. I knew it was good and that I'd helped deliver a little coup.

Sean Spicer — July 2018

In terms of being a Trump protagonist, Sean Spicer really had it all. On his first day as Trump's Press Secretary and Communications Director, just twenty-four hours after the inauguration, he started a shit show, the likes of which we'd never seen before. I was transfixed. Not only was there a hoo-ha about the disappearance of a bust of Martin Luther King – allegedly removed from the new President's office – but there was an unseemly row about inaugura-tion crowd numbers. It got nasty fast. The press were accused of deliberately underestimating the number of spectators; Sean Spicer dug in hard, and he wouldn't let it go. No doubt he'd received an earful that morning, when his boss got wind of the fact that the crowds looked substantially smaller than those that had attended President Obama's inauguration. And so, he found himself making various claims about camera angles, about floor coverings that apparently distorted the numbers. It was shouty and inelegant.

After an unconvincing performance, Trump's right-hand woman, Kellyanne Conway, came to his aid. Or so it seemed. She said that Spicer had presented some new thing called 'alternative facts' – a new kind of truth? We weren't really sure. No one knew what was going on anymore.

It was day one in the Trump White House.

Spicer's demise was swift (although he lasted signifi-cantly longer than the man who replaced him, Anthony 'The Mooch' Scaramucci). He managed a whole six months. Every time he appeared he looked more and more awkward. He became a punching bag of the Left. His credibility was shot. It must have been the longest six months of his life. On 21 July 2017 he resigned. And disappeared into the ether.

And then, inevitably, another 'tell all' book. Although Comey was the more traditional *Newsnight* 'get', I was fixated on convincing Spicer to give us his first book interview. The joy of someone like him was that he was unlikely to be controlled, calm or circumspect. He'd be TV gold. I went after the interview relentlessly and his publisher eventually agreed. We had the exclusive. Emily and I were thrilled. Of course, it couldn't be that straightforward. I should have never relaxed. Just a couple of days before Emily was due to fly to New York to interview him, the email from hell arrived. He didn't want to do that time, perhaps he wouldn't do the interview at all. Usually, I would try to sort all of this alone, but Emily was the kind of presenter who'd help out when things went wrong and so, after some tense emails and fraught phone calls, the two of us made a pincer-like series of calls that, thank god, culminated in an interview. But not in New York. It would be 'down the line' – from the UK studio to Times Square – instead. But it was a win nonetheless.

I was certain this would be spectacular, and so was Emily, but one of the Deputy Editors, Dan Clarke, was

SCOOPS

less convinced. He thought Sean Spicer was yesterday's
man, and a bit of a nobody – a fair position to have – but
it meant he and I disagreed about how long the interview
should be. I was certain that it'd be a showstopper and
asked for fifteen minutes. He thought it would be a damp
squib and suggested five. He was more senior, so it'd be
his decision. Unless Emily got involved. Luckily, she did,
and we settled on fifteen. It turned out to be the right
decision.

The night it aired, I had the opposite of the Schumer
feeling in my gut. When I saw Spicer's face on TV, I just
knew this would be something special.

He had the fixed-on smile of a man who was in the
dock. On the surface everything was great – the suit was a
perfect fit, the hair impeccably neat, the smile wide. But
the tension was everywhere. I was sure Emily could feel it
too. Unlike the US network interviews that he'd already
done – some of which would be fawning or soft – he was
about to get the ride of his life. He just didn't know it yet.

Emily began, 'Sean Spicer joins us live from New York's
Times Square, good evening. Sean, you came to work for
Trump through the Republican Party. You explain in the
book that you're a man who puts party before candidate.
Did you see Donald Trump originally as an awkward fit,
or just what the party needed?'

182

Spicer looked momentarily relieved. 'Thank you, Emily. You know, we had an unbelievable talented group of individuals running to be President. A lot of politicians who were Governors, current and former Senators, and then you had this real estate mogul and reality TV star. By all traditional standards, that's not who kind of made it through. And Trump defied so many of the norms and historical practices that had been part of how you campaigned for President and who becomes the nominee. And so I clearly was not one of those ones who saw it coming initially, but as he wrapped up wins . . . you started to see that he was unique on countless levels.'

Indeed he was. Emily led Spicer through all of the most significant issues – a recent shocking faux pas where Trump appeared to believe President Putin over his own intelligence sources, which some people were calling treason, seemed to pique him a little. 'You were horrified, weren't you?' Emily asked. Spicer's facial response showed he clearly wasn't. 'Emily, like I said, I'm glad he went out and clarified what he meant to say. I think this rush to judgement, always figuring out what . . . with all due respect, telling me what I felt, I've been rather busy the last couple of weeks. I saw it happen, I saw them clean it up and I thought, great, that's what to do, I am glad you

recognise the need to be very clear about what your position is and what our relationship is vis-à-vis Russia.'

It was starting to feel adversarial, especially as Emily
was about to ask about that car crash day – the day after
the inauguration. She went on, 'OK, you make a fair point,
I can't ask you to step into other people's shoes, but you
can perhaps tell us about those first days in the White
House where you found yourself defending the size of
Donald Trump's inauguration crowd on the Mall. Did
you believe what you were saying then?' (We showed the
pictures on screen for emphasis.) 'That the physical crowd
was bigger than Obama's, it was the biggest one ever?'
There was exasperation, verging on scorn, in her voice.

His reply was congenial, but he clearly felt tense. 'Well,
first of all to your point, I appreciate the stroll down
memory lane and the clip. I've been very clear in the book
that if there's a day I would like a do-over on it's that one.
I set the dial that day for a lot of what was to come. I think
what I was trying to do, and clearly not well, was to change
the focus from the number of people attending it to focus
on the total audience that had watched it, and I thought
we were on much safer ground there than trying to focus
on the number of people in the different areas of the
National Mall in Washington.' At this stage he laughed
heartily. 'I did not clearly do a very good job on that and I

talk about it in the book, what we were thinking and what the process was and how hurriedly it all came together. But there's no question that that goes down as one of those days that I'd love a do-over . . . Nobody, Emily, was happy with me that day.' He smiled that opening smile. The smile of a man who has just agreed that he made a fool of himself in his first day on the job. He smiled some more. His response seemed to spur Emily on.

Part of the issue is that the jobs we do – as journalists – are so far removed from what Sean Spicer faced in that role. While he was directly involved in running the most power-ful country on earth, we sat and judged his performance. There's a certain remove we are afforded. We get to come along after and make comments about his performance, about his behaviour, about his capabilities. That tension – between the judged and the judge – was in front of me, on my screen. It was electric, fuelled by Emily's frustration that somehow he wasn't taking what happened seriously enough.

'My point is it became a joke,' she countered, 'it became something that defined you, you joked about it when you presented the Emmy awards, but it wasn't a joke, it was the start of the most corrosive culture. You played with the truth, you led us down a dangerous path, you have corrupted discourse for the entire world by going along with these lies.'

'You have corrupted discourse for the entire world' became a Twitter sensation. Whole articles were written on the interview across the globe, millions of tweets, countless views of the clip. It seemed to encapsulate a frustration that other journalists who spoke to Spicer had been unable to articulate. It went viral. It was the epitome of everything that President Trump would have hated.

Spicer looked annoyed. 'I'm sorry, Emily, you act as though everything began and ended with that. You're taking no accountability for the many false narratives and false stories that the media perpetrated. I wrote a book that I think is a fairly strong representation of what happened in the campaign, the transition and the White House. I take responsibility where I think I'd fallen short or could have done better, but for you to make that kind of claim and make everything sound like it started and ended with Donald Trump is just absolutely ridiculous.'

The President believed he couldn't trust the press, and most of the press believed that they couldn't trust the President. It was an impossible position to reconcile. It only deteriorated as time went on.

He went on to mount a valiant, if weary, attempt to defend his former boss. But his heart wasn't in it. I expected the UK publisher would get an earful as soon as the cameras stopped. I would have been counting the seconds if I were him. If only he'd known about my battle for time, how he'd have wished that the Deputy Editor had won.

Just one more minute on the clock, then he was done. Emily asked him something I was dying to know. 'Would you work for him again?'

Spicer looked defeated and I almost felt sorry for him. 'I think to have worked there under any President, to serve my country, as I've done in so many different ways throughout the years, is an honour that few get and I'm honoured to have been able to do that. It was exhausting, it was tiring, I knew I was becoming the story too often, and I lay this out in the book, that time after time I became the focus and a spokesman should be speaking for somebody else, not having to defend themselves day in and day out.'

Emily persisted. 'Would you go back?' Spicer knew these were his last words. 'I knew the beginning of the end was coming. No. No, I loved being able to do it, I miss the people, but I'll let somebody else do that . . .'

He gave his strained laugh one more time and his voice trailed off. His particular corruption of the discourse was finally over.

Emily, Esme, the Deputy Editor, everyone was relieved. And there was still one more to come.

Stormy Daniels – October 2018

It's a joy of booking interviews that take on a life of their own and present future interview opportunities off their own reputation. The vast amount of coverage that the Sean Spicer interview garnered helped persuade Stormy Daniels' publishers that her first interview should be with us. It was a relatively easy negotiation.

Stormy Daniels – real name Stephanie Gregory Clifford – was an American adult film actress, director and former stripper. She was blonde, glamorous and sexy. She claimed she'd had an affair with Donald Trump in 2006. He denied it. Either way she said there'd been some 'hush money' – a sum of $130,000 from Trump's personal lawyer, Michael Cohen, the signing of an NDA and a promise that she wouldn't talk about the affair publicly. Once he was elected, Daniels filed a lawsuit, saying the NDA was invalid and then, just weeks later, she sat down with America's flagship news programme, *60 Minutes*, and said that she and the President had had sex. Once. The press went wild.

The President denied it, but Daniels did not go quietly. She filed a lawsuit against him, claiming libel for accusing her of being a liar. It was a mess for the President and riveting for the rest of us.

Stormy Daniels was one of my favourite interviews. I've never presumed those who work in the pornography industry are less articulate or credible than other interviewees, even while other coverage of Daniels couldn't look past her profession. In the flesh, Stormy was extremely measured, calm and eloquent. The interview was down the line from the US (that is to say she was in a studio there, while Emily was in our London one) and the backdrop – no doubt fake, put in to make the back of a blank studio wall look more interesting – was some pictures of lush trees and a hillside in the Hollywood Hills. The famous 'Hollywood' sign loomed large over her left shoulder. Her clothing was a striped vest, perfect for the weather where she was, but in stark contrast with our austere London studio and Emily's conservative attire.

Emily didn't shy away from what would have previously been mortifying. Trump's time in office had meant we'd had to become adept at dealing with phrases like 'pussy-grabbing' and 'golden showers with Russian prostitutes'. This was no time for coyness. 'In the book you've gone into quite intimate details about how the President has sex. Why did you do that?' she asked.

Daniels responded, 'To prove that I was telling the truth, so that, you know, actually I don't make it a habit to kiss and tell. Part of me feels guilty about doing that, but by recounting every detail I think it's obvious that I know things that only someone who actually experienced and been there would know. And I would never have included any of those things as a "kiss and tell" for lack of a better explanation, if it wasn't for the fact that I was being called a liar.'

To me, the best parts of her book were the excruciating sexual details. Her motivation seemed clear – to provide so much information about his physiology that those who shared her knowledge would know she was telling the truth. Although it wasn't articulated in the interview, the book, *Full Disclosure*, did exactly that. If you're a little more strait-laced, skip the rest of this paragraph. In it she describes the President's penis as 'smaller than average' but 'not freakishly small'. The lines that stayed in public consciousness the most are when she writes, 'He knows he has an unusual penis . . . It has a huge mushroom head. Like a toadstool.' And, just like that, Trump's 'mushroom penis' became a topic of international debate.

Emily approached it in a less direct way. 'Many of us thought the world couldn't get much crazier and yet here we are in 2018, hearing descriptions about the shape of the President's penis. Was that all part of the truth telling or was the aim there to, on one level, just humiliate him?'

Daniels was resolute. 'No, of course not, I would never humiliate someone for no reason. Or for any reason. I mean, that's body shaming or sex shaming or betrayal, and it was that he attacked me first. I was called a liar, that it never happened, and unless he's had a penis transplant then I am pretty sure that's a checkmate.'

I stifled a laugh. It was! It felt like they'd messed with the wrong woman. The NDA, the hush money, it had all become irrelevant as soon as Trump became President. Otherwise, their fling would have been just that. Now? It was another Trump scandal. But Daniels refused to let the narrative about her persist. That's what I loved about her. Here she was, facing one of our most famous interrogators, having been the recipient of ridicule and censure, and she was completely holding her own.

Emily played devil's advocate. 'People have read and heard your story and I guess it's easy for them to say, look, the encounter was a transaction, you both knew the way the world worked . . . that you were hoping to get a part on *The Apprentice*, you knew what you were getting into originally when you were looking for fame and fortune, it's no surprise that you would end up getting hurt in that situation.'

Daniels refused to capitulate again. 'It was a very consensual encounter. I was *not* paid that night, I was *not* offered money, it was *not* prostitution, but yes, it was two consenting adults, he mentioned something about a part on a TV show. It was never specifically said, "Hey, if you have sex with me I will give you this." It wasn't anything like that. But it was definitely not a "MeToo" moment. That's another really irritating thing when people think I was either a prostitute or a victim. I was neither.'

It was rare to hear someone rejecting the opportunity to be a 'victim'. We were in the full midst of the #MeToo era. Every day there seemed to be another sad tale of man as aggressor, woman as victim. It was refreshing to hear her narrative. She wasn't a victim. She just wanted the world to know that she wasn't a liar. Even if the actual President of the United States said so.

As it happened, a whole other tale of sexual mores had just been played out. Earlier in the year, President Trump had nominated Brett Kavanaugh to be a justice in the Supreme Court. A few weeks later Christine Blasey Ford, a professor, alleged that Kavanaugh had sexually assaulted her when they were both in high school. She was fifteen. He was seventeen. The whole thing played out like some terrible reality show. She went public. He denied it. Inevitably, there was a tweet from Trump, saying that if her allegations were true, either she or her parents would have reported it at the time. Trial by Twitter. By September, the Senate Judiciary Committee was involved. Were the allegations true? Was this man fit for one of the highest offices in the land? Blasey Ford gave her evidence. We all watched in the *Newsnight* office. The level of scrutiny was agonising. It was exactly the kind of scrutiny Stormy Daniels had also faced in the court of public opinion.

Emily made the connection directly. 'Christine Blasey Ford gave her testimony last week. We've heard from the "porn star", we've heard from "the professor". Is there any difference ultimately as to whether your testimonies are believed?'

I winced a little at the distinction. It was a fair question, but it felt like a judgement. Daniels responded, 'I think that people are quicker to discredit and discount me because I work in the adult business. For some reason people think that sex workers, which includes strippers, porn stars, porn producers, somehow don't know right from wrong and are less human. I experience it every day. They for some reason think that because of my job I am to be trusted less than someone who is like a schoolteacher or an accountant.'

In fact, the Senate Judiciary Committee had voted down party lines, and, despite 'The Professor's' testimony, they'd voted 11–10 to allow Kavanaugh to advance his confirmation to a full Senate vote. By 6 October, the full Senate confirmed him by a vote of 50–48. Blasey Ford's public scrutiny had been in vain. Emily continued with the comparison. 'But I guess what we have seen proves the opposite, doesn't it? Christine Blasey Ford, who is an academic and a professor, still wasn't believed by many Republicans either.'

We were almost out of time and Stormy was the perfect interviewee. Open, easy to understand, and she also did something that was so rare – she actually answered questions directly. 'Exactly, but I think that she has more support from other women. I am very grateful to all the women who have stood up and supported me, but some of the nastiest comments I have gotten are from other women who think that I am not worth believing or I am inhuman because I work in the adult business, and my job should not have anything to do with my character.'

Time was up. Just one more thing to ask. 'How do you think Trump will be remembered as a President?'

Daniels relaxed. She laughed and replied, 'I think time will only tell, it's not over yet.'

Indeed, it wasn't. There were two more years of drama to come.

9

Walkouts: Steven Seagal

Despite the constant need for content, it takes monumental efforts to actually get anything on air at the BBC. Not because of the technicalities of television itself (though they are challenging enough) but because of an idiosyncratic internal commissioning process for certain programmes. As an outsider, I'd always assumed it went something like this. Producer: 'Here's an idea for something, do you like it?' Boss: 'No, it's rubbish, don't bother' or 'Yes, that sounds great, go get it!'

If only.

It's a long, arduous and frustrating process. And one that I spent a lot of my professional life trying to conquer. Ideally without losing my temper or walking out of the building (proper strops: 2; mini-strops: impossible to count).

Broadly, the process for *Newsnight* was as follows. We'd all collect various ideas for guests (in my case, screenshotting anything I was drawn to on my days off) and then we'd 'pitch' them for the planning meeting on Mondays. Suggestions could be as eclectic as you liked, from the bleeding obvious – Prince Harry, Meghan Markle, the Pope – to the wonderfully obscure – a theatre director no one had heard of, the soon-to-be leader of a small country, or an important philosopher or photographer who might appeal to the *Newsnight* viewer. Really you're looking for newsworthiness, intellectual or artistic heft or something purely entertaining, though this was rarer. So, stage one is getting it through that meeting.

After the meeting, you'd start busting a gut to actually deliver the suggestions you'd made. Naturally, the more you suggest ideas, the more work you create for yourself. But I couldn't help myself. I was competitive. Week after week, month after month, year after year, I'd mean to reduce the number I would suggest, and never ever managed to do it. Even in the last couple of weeks of my BBC career, I'd still come with an impossible list.

If you actually managed to convince the person to take part, you'd assume that was the end of it, right? But news moves fast, so sometimes a person who was relevant on

Monday is irrelevant by Tuesday, or another programme would grab them first, and they'd fall off the list.

The thing that I found impossible was when that didn't happen – you'd managed to convince the guest, they were still relevant, they'd agreed to give us the 'exclusive', but then, because of the manoeuvrings of the *Newsnight* hierarchy, I would often have to start all over again convincing members of my own team to put out the content that I'd already convinced a Deputy Editor to allow, bearing in mind the guest would have already committed. It was extremely frustrating. Each day's programme was run by an EOD – editor of the day – and he or she was more senior than me and often had autonomy over the content. So, you could spend weeks getting something agreed, then they'd decide to drop it at the last second, against all pleading and protestation. Or you'd have to convince them on the day. Or get the Deputy Editor to put their foot down and insist it went on, if they were willing to do so. Worst case, you'd have to call someone you'd been dealing with for weeks, maybe even months, and then tell them that the thing you'd told them was super important and definitely wanted was now unimportant and unwanted. It was the worst part of the job. It could be humiliating, and made the programme look bad. Sometimes, after fuming in the toilet or ranting to a colleague, I had to call upon someone more senior to beg: 'It's five minutes of TV! Can we just do it?!'

The two proper strops concerned Dennis Rodman (the volatile US basketball star) and Prince Albert of Monaco (the never out of the news son of Grace Kelly). The former had just returned from North Korea, where he'd become the new best friend of Kim Jong Un. Their unlikely friendship made global headlines. The pictures of them shooting the breeze, laughing, high-fiving and embracing were astonishing. I had the exclusive. Live. In the Vatican's St Peter's Square. My editor wouldn't run it. I couldn't believe it. I saw red. I may have shouted. I was so livid that I had to leave the building.

And Prince Albert? I'd scored an interview with him just before I left the BBC, and he was going to talk about oceans, but also about the monarchy and Meghan and Harry. I knew it would make headlines galore but, for complex reasons and a couple of miscommunications, my own programme didn't want to run it. This time, I didn't drop it. I refused to. Instead, I took it to the brilliant BBC *World News* presenter, Yalda Hakim. She loved it, we did it, and the global headlines – where he said Meghan and Harry should have kept their dissatisfaction private – were the most extensive that I'd had since the Prince Andrew interview. The *Spectator* called me 'the Royal

Family's nemesis' as a result. My judgement – and my strop – had been vindicated.

Sometimes, you'd get past every single one of these hurdles and then the guest themselves would drop out at the last second (heartbreaking), or another broadcaster would grab them and you'd be forced to try to convince your team that going second was still worth it.

Sometimes, just sometimes, you'd manage to get past all of those hurdles, setbacks and internal machinations, and find someone who everyone agreed on. Who would be the perfect heady mix of famous, newsworthy, important, interesting, great TV and, crucially, that no one on the team would ever suggest dropping.

That someone was Steven Seagal. Yes, the Hollywood martial arts mega star. He'd gained fame in the 1980s and 1990s, most famously in the film *Under Siege*. Not content with being a martial arts movie star, latterly Seagal had begun a foray into law enforcement and politics. He was a Reserve Deputy Chief in the Louisiana Sheriff's Office. I don't know what that meant in terms of actual responsibility but imagine someone's face if they got pulled over and Steven Seagal appeared. You'd be hard pressed not to laugh, panic or run. Probably all three.

As well as his dealings in law enforcement, Seagal had links to Russia. He somehow became pally with Vladimir

Putin. They shared a love of martial arts. Seagal's expertise in aikido matched Putin's love of judo. He was granted Russian citizenship in 2016. He was a vocal supporter of the Russian President and the two of them were pictured together. It was one of those surreal friendships that can only happen when one of you is a world leader and the other is a movie star. It was my Kim Jong Un/Dennis Rodman 2.0.

In 2018, President Putin appointed Seagal as a 'special envoy' to improve ties with the United States. The Russian Foreign Ministry made the announcement on social media, explaining that the role was unpaid but similar to that of a United Nations 'goodwill ambassador'. He'd be expected to promote US–Russia relations in the humanitarian sphere. It was too good to ignore!

To be honest, I thought he'd be hard to convince. As well as his Russian duties, he had a string of allegations of sexual misconduct made against him. They'd started in the 1990s and resurfaced in the era of #MeToo – the actress Portia de Rossi made an allegation in a tweet: 'My final audition for a Steven Seagal movie took place in his office. He told me how important it was to have chemistry off-screen as he sat me down and unzipped his leather pants. I ran out and called my agent.' She wasn't the only one to make allegations against him.

British actress Rachel Grant claimed she lost a role because she refused his advances. The allegations were refuted by Seagal but they were out there and he could be sure we would address them in an interview. Yet somehow his agent said yes.

I'm always clear to interviewees that we will ask about their latest project or role as well as, crucially, 'other news related issues'. We are a news programme in a democracy. It's not in the public interest to have agreed-upon questions posed. We decline when asked for them. We barely provide topic areas. If you assent to an interview, it's not a forum for you then to try to restrict an open conversation, however much people may push for it. Most of what we will ask is infinitely predictable. I'm always bemused when interviewees don't see something coming. One time Eric Schmidt, the former CEO of Google, seemed surprised that we asked him about the company's tax affairs. The CEO of Coca-Cola appeared perplexed when we challenged him about the sugar content of the drinks. It would be like having David Cameron on and not asking about Brexit. And so, of course, after talking about Russia, Seagal would be expecting to speak about the other issues. It was the middle of the #MeToo movement. He was one of many men being accused of impropriety. It could not be more newsworthy.

Kirsty Wark was presenting that evening in October 2018. We were all looking forward to the exclusive. It would be intriguing to hear about his new political sympathies but also a rare chance to ask him, on camera, about the allegations. We pencilled in an extended slot. I worried he'd be a no-show and didn't allow myself to relax until he was sitting and mic'd.

When he arrived, I was relieved, and somewhat surprised. He was an imposing figure. Broad shouldered, his body filled the screen. The backdrop for the interview was a hastily booked venue somewhere in Russia that suited him well. The room was dark and shadowy; it hadn't seen daylight in years. A large bookshelf, filled with rows of leather-bound books, dominated the right of the screen. Perhaps encyclopaedias. Seagal himself was dressed all in black. Black hair. Black moustache. Black beard. He wore small, elliptical, yellow-tinted glasses.

The assumption was that he'd be monosyllabic and difficult to interview. This assumption would prove right.

Kirsty looked her usual positive self. We had ten minutes with him. I was eagerly anticipating every moment. 'Talking about your relationship with Vladimir Putin, how did you first meet?'

Seagal's voice was exactly as you'd imagine. A low timbre, a little halting, economical, somewhat lacking in the usual easy articulation of the average *Newsnight* guest. He began, 'Well, um, I really don't remember the exact circumstances but I believe there was some kind of an event where several different foreign diplomats and different important people were in Moscow and, errr, I was invited to his home at that point and from there we really started talking about the martial arts and had some sort of similar interests. And from there we became a little bit, you know, closer and closer friends.'

It didn't get any less awkward from there. We were about a minute in. Things went from cordial to stilted to frosty by question three. Kirsty was gentle, but firm. 'But he has obviously asked you to take on this role as special envoy to foster good relations between your two countries. This is a very difficult role for you just now.'

Segal looked very serious. 'It is. It's, errr, relations are very strained at the moment. To be honest with you, not to try to throw any softballs to myself or anybody else, in the beginning I am really thinking about cultural things that may help us, you know, get into meaningful dialogue. Just about things that are not necessarily hot potatoes and difficult political issues, you know.'

In my head the 'cultural things' could only be martial arts. I imagined a large ring, geopolitics style, where, instead of diplomacy, adversaries would grapple one another until one side won. Putin would take on Obama. Bets would be placed. Or perhaps he meant mass screenings of his films, dubbed into Russian, where both countries could sit side by side, sharing popcorn, to foster better international relations. Ideally there'd be horse riding or bear wrestling. Maybe they'd just all share some vodka with a Big Mac. He didn't elaborate.

He didn't elaborate much in any of his answers. Kirsty was working hard to get content. We were already two minutes in. 'If you had to choose, though, that would be very hard, between your Russian citizenship and your American citizenship, what would you do?' Seagal's face didn't seem to convey many expressions other than stern, very stern or extremely stern, but he looked a bit annoyed. 'Well, certainly I am not going to have to choose, so that's a moot point.'

He was about to get more irritated. 'But, you obviously spend a lot of time in Russia, you spend a lot of time in America, you're making films and so forth. And in terms of your life in America you've been very much caught up in all of the allegations of sexual harassment. You had a rape allegation against you, and I wonder how you deal with all that?'

I held my breath. He *must* have known this would be asked. He must have prepared his denial. He must have had an answer at the tip of his tongue. I expected him to trot it out. To make his position and his refutation clear. To refuse to go into details and then to insist we move on. To get back to his preferred topic.

Instead, as Kirsty was asking her question – right around the moment she said the word 'rape' – he pulled his earpiece out, got up and walked out of shot. The chair was empty, the books were left on the shelves all alone.

Ever the professional, Kirsty made it clear that he'd made previous denials. 'Steven Seagal there, and although he didn't respond there, he has previously said that he denies any allegations that have been made against him.'

Three minutes and four seconds. That's how long he lasted.

After the interview, a slew of networks picked it up. It was all over TMZ and the US networks. One of the women who had accused him thanked us on Twitter. The clip was watched hundreds of thousands of times. Inadvertently, he'd made the allegations big news all over again.

His assistant called me. He was worried he'd lose his job. I hoped this wasn't true but could not apologise for the question. Why Seagal hadn't considered it – and why he had squandered the opportunity to respond to allegations – was not our responsibility.

His strop was now global news.

At least my strops never made headlines.

10

Prince Andrew:
The Negotiations

Wednesday 20 November 2019 –– BREAKING: Prince Andrew to step down from royal duties for the near future: 'I have asked Her Majesty if I may step back from public duties for the foreseeable future, and she has given her permission.'

As I stood, alone, before Buckingham Palace in May of 2019, waiting for the armed police to let me across the cobbled courtyard for the first time, I would have never dreamed that, only six months later, Prince Andrew's reputation would be shot to pieces and his life as a serving member of the Royal Family would be over.

I had no concept of what might happen and little hope the negotiations would get me anywhere. As far as I knew,

no member of the Royal Family had ever even been on
Newsnight. We had no connections in the Palace. We'd
had no meetings with any part of the royal communications network. It was rare that we ever even did a 'royal'
story – only the death of Diana, the death of the Queen
Mother, the royal weddings of William and Kate, Meghan
and Harry. In essence only huge national events that we
could not ignore. There was a certain reluctance to cover
them. Given the vast and unremitting coverage of these
kind of events across the network, it could be hard to
establish the *Newsnight* 'take'. So, we'd end up with some
esoteric debate, probably with Simon Schama, about the
long view on the British monarchy, or the possibility of
Prince Charles as King Charles, or the merits of the
hereditary line, or which Crown dependencies were
about to disappear next, or whether a constitutional
monarchy was sustainable. It was not something we had
great specialism in. As such, it was not our strong suit.

Other BBC presenters and programmes had been
specifically called upon to do royal interviews – most
famously during my time, Mishal Husain conducted
Meghan and Harry's engagement interview in 2017. On
that occasion I believe, though I don't know for sure, that
she had been specifically requested. So, someone in the
BBC leadership would have received a call or an approach.

There were no months of graft. No uncertainty. No competition. I couldn't even imagine what that was like – I had to work so hard for content. I had never even taken a call of that kind from the Royal Family.

In the same year, *Today* on Radio 4 scored a coup – Prince Harry was their guest editor for a day. They had cemented their position as having the best royal connections and interviews. We had none.

And so, this was my first ever foray into dealing with anyone in the Royal Household. Little did I know it would also be my last.

It had all started innocuously – an email from a PR to me in November 2018, suggesting a chat about Pitch@Palace, Prince Andrew's initiative to support entrepreneurs around the world. Would *Newsnight* like to interview him about his work? The simple answer was 'no' – the offer was just to talk about the competition Pitch@Palace was running and, as you now know, we won't ever agree to talk 'just' about one thing or allow interviewees to give conditions. We refuse to air puff pieces that advertise an interviewee's pet project and are fiercely proud of our editorial independence. So, I politely declined that offer, unless we could also ask about all of the things we were interested in – Brexit, the future of the monarchy, Harry and Meghan and the supposed tensions in the Royal Family. Unsurprisingly, the answer was a firm 'no'. 'Do come back to me if the position changes!' I signed off. It seemed so unlikely that I didn't even tell my boss. What was the point? I assumed I would never hear from them again.

But then, six months later, I did.

In May 2019, they got back in touch – Prince Andrew was now open to a broader chat, and one that wouldn't have any parameters, would I be interested in learning more? Absolutely, I would. And so I had a chat with the PR, setting out once again how we wouldn't ever allow conditions or terms or provide questions if an interview was agreed – it's always best to land that to avoid any misunderstandings later on. The PR took it all in, and agreed to talk to the Palace, and get right back to me. She told me she needed to talk to Prince Andrew's private secretary, Amanda Thirsk, and she would be back in touch later. It was the first time I had ever heard Amanda's name and I immediately googled her. She sounded, and looked, suitably impressive – a woman who had worked for the Prince for seven years, but who had previously had a successful career as a banker in the City, a Cambridge graduate, a trusted and senior member of his (small) staff.

To be honest, I wrote it off as another dead end and went back to my daily work. I still didn't even mention it to my boss. But, shortly after, the PR emailed me back saying that the Palace was still open to meeting for a chat, and would I like to come in the following week to meet with Amanda and see if an interview might be viable?

I'm not going to lie – I was excited to go.

I wasn't even nervous at this stage. Perhaps that was helpful. I approached it as a useful meeting and an introduction to a relationship with the Royal Household. At this stage I wasn't hoping to land an interview out of it. I couldn't quite fathom why Prince Andrew would particularly want to talk to us – after all, even before all of the Epstein accusations, it's not an easy ride. The beauty of *Newsnight* is the brilliant in-depth interviews, with nowhere to hide. This serves as a powerful disincentive for those with skeletons stowed away in their closets.

You have to remember the situation in 2019 was very different to the one now. Jeffrey Epstein wasn't a name that rang bells for a lot of people. The allegations against him, and his 'friendship' with Prince Andrew, barely registered in the UK news at the time. I imagine most people on the programme wouldn't have even known about the association; it was so far removed. Although Epstein had been arrested and convicted of a couple of sexual offences a decade earlier, and his association with the Prince had caused some uncomfortable questions at Davos, it wasn't yet something of note. And Epstein hadn't yet faced arrest for the slew of sex trafficking offences, as he did later that year. But, as an ex-criminal barrister, the case was always at the back of my mind. So, I had checked Prince Andrew's last comments on the case and remembered them.

I love being well prepped in every negotiation, and I hate to be caught off guard, so I started to work on it seriously – planning, making calls and doing full background research on Amanda and on Prince Andrew. I wanted to cover every possible eventuality. Then I tried to work out what their sweet spot for doing the interview would be, and what the barriers to agreeing were, and then formulated my responses to them. Although I hadn't heard of Amanda Thirsk before, I knew a couple of friends who likely had, and who had also met Prince Andrew, and so I checked in with them to get an idea of who I would be meeting. The picture that came back was of someone who was entirely my ideal kind of person to negotiate with – they said that she was formidable, clever, thorough, sharp, fiercely loyal to Prince Andrew, and didn't suffer fools gladly. I hoped not to be a fool, and did proper reading on what the Prince had been up to recently, and the topics I felt were most newsworthy that she might ask me about. Those meetings can veer all over the place – you never know what you're going to be asked, or what issues might arise.

The first negotiation –
22 May 2019

Arriving at the Palace was surreal. I've lived in London for decades, and must have passed by on foot, or on the bus, thousands of times. In fact, as one of those Londoners who never does 'touristy things', I hadn't even stopped outside the place since I was a small child. I'd never been to stand with the crowds for a royal wedding, or place flowers for a royal death. I had never even seen the Changing of the Guard. And now, here I was, standing outside the imposing façade, trying to work out where on earth to go. All I could see was a load of armed police at one entrance, an open gate, and I couldn't believe you could just walk in that way, but that's exactly what happened. I went and asked where to go; they looked me up on a list, took my ID and rang through to someone who sanctioned my entry. And so, the sea of police and guns parted, and I began the long walk across the cobbled courtyard to the Palace's door. The hundreds and hundreds of tourists stacked up against the Palace gates stared at and past me as I traipsed across the cobbles, somewhat impeded by a perilously high pair of boots. As

I walked, a fully decked-out member of Palace staff, all black and gold, stood beaming at me from the entrance. It felt like an eternity getting to him, and then he beckoned me in.

I am always super early so I had time to take in the details. The waiting room was tiny but immaculate – filled with the kinds of ornate furniture that I love, and a teeny mantelpiece with a large golden gilt mirror and a dark wooden, loudly ticking clock. The mantel was made of white marble, with flecks of grey. To the left, a plush gilt chair, a bit like the cheap knock-off I had in my bedroom, sat snugly in the corner next to a small, dark wooden table. It looked like a little writing desk; like something you'd find in a romantic Parisian hotel. Underneath it was a little glass box, with a small silver model of an aeroplane inside. Above it, a jaunty watercolour of a beautiful white horse, flanked by some top hatted man with a crop, encased in an elaborate thick gilt frame. Next to me, on a tiny table, sat a blue and white vase and a framed picture of Her Majesty, in a yellow jacket and hat, holding some brightly coloured blooms, smiling and surveying the room. As I was in there alone, and feeling daring, I picked the frame up and took a closer look at the monarch's semi-smiling face. The frame wasn't heavy. It looked like a cheap, black wooden frame from Ikea – it was somehow strangely discordant with the surrounding splendour. I swiftly put it back, in case I dropped it and got thrown out before I had even begun. Elsewhere on the table, there were a couple of royal themed books and accoutrements.

I loved being in there, all alone, listening to the chatter of the staff about some royal visit to Sainsbury's, and watching a soldier come in and remove his huge bearskin cap, and have a chat for a moment about the day. From what I could hear, it seemed that the Queen was in the Palace today, but was about to leave, and everyone was busying themselves with whatever arrangements needed to be made for that. As they darted in and out organising things, I remembered that I still had my phone with me and grabbed a quick picture of my shoes on the royal carpet (cream, with what looked like green mini-shamrocks or splodges of some kind) and then, feeling bolder, I may have sneaked a selfie in the Palace mirror. Maybe two! It was naughty, but irresistible. I could show them to my mum sometime. She'd love that. They'd remain my little secret photo album. Then, I sat and waited, as the two PRs who were accompanying me arrived, and we swapped pleasantries and waited to be summoned upstairs. I was back to my professional self.

The Palace was being refurbished at the time – I suspect it's an endless task, given its age and size – and when we were collected, we were taken in old-fashioned lifts, upstairs, past huge busts of former Kings and Queens, and through swathes of empty corridors.

Amanda's office was at the end of a long corridor: a small room, peppered with pictures of Prince Andrew and his family. And it was then that it all really sunk in – I was here, in the Queen's 'house', about to pitch for the first royal interview I'd ever asked for. The nerves finally hit me.

Amanda was exactly as I had been told – impeccable manners, thorough and direct, and every word mattered, never glib. Not a hair out of place, beautiful jewellery; the kind of effortless, classy chic that I have never managed to master – I was sporting leather trousers and unruly curls. As ever, the space between what I had been told – that Prince Andrew was now open to a general interview with no conditions – and what I was told when actually speaking to Amanda was significant, but we talked for two hours, and it looked like I had managed to convince her that our way – a fully open conversation with no conditions or subjects off the table – was the way to go. I'd started off being told that he would only talk about Pitch@Palace and entrepreneurism, but, by the end, we agreed that it would encompass all of the kinds of news issues that we would want to ask about – Brexit, baby

Archie and the impact of the arrival of Meghan on the Royal Family, the future of the monarchy and the place of the UK in the world – as well as any other relevant issues that arose at the time of the interview. That wonderful feeling of closing a deal was swelling inside me. It finally felt real. But then, Amanda said there was one red line – the issue of his friendship with Epstein was old news, and she was clear that we couldn't ask about it if we agreed to the interview. My heart sank. I explained that we never agree to terms or red lines, but she was insistent. I launched into one of my speeches about the freedom of the press and the duties of a public service broadcaster, hoping to persuade her, but it was clear that this was a non-negotiable. So, I did the 'holding pattern' thing, and said I would go back and discuss it with my Editor, knowing full well we would 100% never ever agree, but hoping that Amanda might change her mind in the interim.

She didn't.

We had to decline the interview. She took it well. And so, Prince Andrew went on ITV instead. I don't know what their conversations were, but they didn't ask about Epstein in that broadcast. It was painful to watch 'my' interview on another channel. It was such a shame to be so close, and to miss out. My first foray in

SCOOPS

the world of royal interviews had failed. I assumed that was that.

This was in May 2019. Eight weeks later, Jeffrey Epstein was arrested. Twelve weeks later, he was dead. Twenty weeks later, I had managed to persuade Amanda that Prince Andrew's position – of silence in the face of global scrutiny – was untenable. And so, on Monday 28 October, as the world clamoured to hear from him, Amanda agreed to meet me again.

The second negotiation – 28 October 2019

I had stayed in touch with Amanda since Epstein's arrest, and knew that the trust and mutual respect between us, and our rapport, gave me a formidable advantage over other broadcasters. It was hard not to message every few days, following major and minor developments in the story, and then email her again,

218

and again, and again. I'm constantly negotiating that fine line between professional commitment and becoming a total pain in the arse. At this stage, I was still pretty sure His Royal Highness would never agree to speak with us, but I needed to stay in the game just in case. Some colleagues thought that the hope of an interview was wildly deluded. They even sent me jokey emails, asking if I had got an interview with Prince Andrew 'yet'. These spurred me on.

The situation was escalating fast. Not only had Epstein died in what some thought were suspicious circumstances, but the full scale of his destructive behaviour was starting to come into sharp focus. And that of Prince Andrew's other friend – Ghislaine Maxwell. The extraordinary Virginia Roberts Giuffre, and other victims, started to speak, and we also knew that colleagues at Channel 4's *Dispatches* were working on a programme on Prince Andrew, with a *Panorama* due to follow, including a possible interview with Virginia herself.

The written statements the Palace gave on Prince Andrew's behalf made his silence more and more deafening.

Initially, Amanda didn't agree to another meeting, but I persisted and, as the pressure on the Prince rose, she finally agreed, five months after our first chat, on 28 October. I was actually on leave – it was half term and my son was with his dad – and I was meant to be going for some overpriced spa day. But I immediately cancelled it all. As before, I assumed this would be my last visit to the Palace, and I wanted to make the most of it.

In that vein, I did something I had never done before – I decided to take someone with me to the negotiation. I'd done every negotiation in my career alone, but this time, feeling we could actually be close to something monumental, I decided to ask Emily Maitlis to come with me. I was lucky to have a presenter who trusts my judgement implicitly, and I knew that Emily's star power, in person, could really help seal the deal. She instantly agreed. The fact I had never asked before raised the stakes all round. It was possibly the chance of a lifetime, or maybe a waste of her time. Of course, she was willing to play those odds.

Although Emily's presence strengthened my hand, I found it strangely restrictive. I'm used to speaking freely, but I had to ensure I didn't dominate the conversation, didn't jump in too fast, didn't swear or say anything that could be seen as controversial, and that I looked to Emily to speak first in areas that were more relevant to her. In a negotiation I was always in charge. I wasn't 'just' the producer. I was autonomous and free to speak as I wished. There was no hierarchy or office dynamics to worry about. I wasn't used to having to share, or to defer. This new situation made me a little uncomfortable at first. I'm sure Emily felt the same way. But we adapted quickly. That time together would prove hugely helpful in working out the subtleties of future negotiations. We were a good team.

We fell into a rhythm – I answered the questions relating to editorial issues and practicalities (venue, timings, length of interview) and provided the constant thrust of persuasion, repeating my central mantra – that Prince Andrew needed to be accountable and say something on camera or be presumed guilty – over and over in a multitude of ways. Emily covered all of the practical 'presenter' questions and about why she was best placed to conduct this interview. I tried to work out if this was an exploratory conversation, or if there really was an interview to be had. The questions were general enough that it could still have been theoretical.

No conditions were suggested, no red flags. As we neared the end of the conversations, I dared to ask, 'You seem to be leaning towards doing an interview of some kind. Can you confirm that's the case?' I held my breath as I waited for Amanda's reply. I glimpsed Emily doing the same. It felt like an age passed. 'Yes,' she replied, 'and if we do, it will only be one. Ever.'

We both exhaled, exchanged glances and left.

As it happened, it was Changing of the Guard that day, and we had to be led through the bowels of the Palace to get out. Past old posters and piles of washing, past fading photos and decorative tables, until it felt like we might never leave. I took everything in, knowing it would be the only time I was in this underground place and made a mental note of all of the mundanities of Palace life. Of course, this time I couldn't take photos, and so I committed those light stone walls to my memory, took in every detail to enjoy in my personal memory bank. It was an extraordinary route out. The contrast with the splendour and pomp of the floor above was quite something. I'd never really thought about the royal laundry before, or where the royal loo roll might be kept. It felt like being inside a far more intimate part of Palace life than anything we had seen before. I looked left and right the whole walk out, desperate not to miss a thing. A single random cardboard box or an abandoned magazine, a couple of royal posters, an empty display cabinet. Then, finally, we were outside. Thrust through a back door into the cold London air.

We were both discombobulated. From the adrenaline, and also because we didn't really know where we were anymore. Emily looked for a cab, we briefly exchanged views. We both knew we had a chance. Emily rushed to the office, and I called my Deputy Editor, Stewart Maclean. Knowing I tend not to oversell a situation, he asked me if I thought they might do something, and whether we had a genuine chance. Although I could barely believe it myself, I heard myself say 'Yes!' I knew we had something real here. It was no longer a figment of my own optimism.

This was the moment that something in me switched. I started to feel anxious, not the all-consuming kind, but the low-level variety that hums in the background, that stops you from falling asleep straight away, and becomes the first thing you think of every morning. The hope of winning, tinged with the more plausible reality that you could lose. And then I'd have to live with that 'nearly' moment forever.

Twelve long days later we got the email we had all hoped for. It arrived from Amanda, early on a Saturday morning, 9 November: could Emily, Stew and I come to the Palace in two days? Prince Andrew wanted to meet with us.

The final negotiation –
Monday 11 November 2021

Nothing prepares you for turning up at Buckingham Palace to meet Prince Andrew to discuss a potential interview about his friendship with a serious sex offender. It was Stew's first time at the Palace, and I could sense his excitement. Emily and I were most concerned about how to greet the Prince, and a kind member of the Palace staff hurriedly taught us the 'curtsy' – more of a head bob in my case. It kept us nicely distracted for a few moments, as we practised the right combination of bob and leg movements, while trying not to fall over in our respective shoes (high heels for Emily, snakeskin boots for me). I hadn't slept a wink all weekend. I'd been prepping, reading, talking to people who had met Prince Andrew to gauge how to approach him. Then I had been rehearsing possible questions in my head, thinking about what their sticking points would be, gaming every possible calibration and option. Thinking ahead. Thinking non-stop. I'd been obsessing. I didn't usually get like this. My son Lucas, now thirteen, had even noticed. 'You OK, Mum?' I wasn't.

That morning, on the way to work, I'd done something new. The kind of thing I would usually laugh at. I'd done affirmations. Well, more precisely, I had, under my breath, kept repeating the phrase 'You've f***ing got this, Sam!' Over and over. I must have looked demented, striding along the streets of Hammersmith. By the time I returned that evening to make bolognese, my life could be different.

This time, when I arrived at the Palace, things were stricter – our phones were taken and everything felt much more formal.

From my research and conversations, I was confident that Prince Andrew would be fun to negotiate with. He seemed open, confident, energetic, boisterous and thick-skinned and so I had assumed that, despite the circum-stances, the negotiation would likely be good natured. I could take a few risks in my tone, possibly even some banter. It would all come down to trust. And who he felt most comfortable with. I'd be 100% myself. This wasn't, in my view, a time to be conservative. We had no clue how many people they were still speaking to. No idea who else might come to the Palace before or after us. I wanted to leave with no regrets. I also hoped I had an extra advan-tage that likely no one else would have. I'd actually repre-sented people accused of the kinds of crimes we were

talking about here. I had direct experience of alleged sex
offenders, rapists, traffickers. I knew what was at stake –
he was a man who could be facing a swathe of litigation
and that is a terrifying place to be.

We all distracted ourselves. In my case, trying not to
sweat even more profusely with nerves (I *do* sweat). And
we waited for what felt like an age (about ten minutes) to
be summoned upstairs. We went, with hearts in our
mouths, back into that small room that I had first gone
into, alone, all those months ago. Amanda was there to
greet us and said that His Royal Highness would be along
shortly. We sat down on the dark wooden chairs. The
room was snug. I was directly next to Emily and Emily
was next to the empty chair at the head of the table. The
one where, shortly, a member of the Royal Family would
sit, a few feet away. I knew I'd probably never get to do
anything like this ever again. I waited. Concentrated on
my breathing. Wished I'd worn something smarter. We
congregated by the doorway. Standing. Waiting for him to
arrive. Thinking through the royal bob. Trying to remember the correct form of address – 'Your Royal Highness'
the first time, 'Sir' in the interactions thereafter. A haze of
nerves, hope, determination.

Suddenly, he appeared, from around the corner of the
short corridor: 'Morning!' His voice was upbeat. He was

smiling. He seemed friendly. 'I hope you don't mind, but I brought someone with me!' This was not something that any of us had expected to hear. We exchanged glances. Who could it be? A lawyer? Someone else in communications? Maybe someone from the Queen's staff?

And then, from behind him, Princess Beatrice appeared.

To be frank, the only thing worse than speaking to a prospective interviewee about allegations of sexual impropriety, paedophilia and sex with a seventeen-year-old girl is having to do so in front of his daughter. Princess Beatrice was polite and engaged, carrying a notebook and a pen, but she was evidently anxious about the meeting, unlike her father. The atmosphere palpably changed for us all. In that moment, I had to make a split-second decision – who would be the person who had the most impact on the final outcome of this negotiation? Of course, the decision was for Prince Andrew, but it was clear that he was already thinking about who he would choose to speak to, rather than whether he would choose to speak at all, and we already thought that Amanda seemed keen for him to speak with a heavyweight interviewer, like Emily, rather than risk being accused of choosing someone who would give him an 'easy time'. But Princess Beatrice was a total curveball. I had heard she was close to the Queen, who might well ask for her opinion on the meeting, and also knew that she was very close to her father and was clearly there to protect his interests and to ensure that we were the right people to speak to. In an imaginary meeting that I envisaged after this, the Queen would turn to Andrew and ask him how it went. He'd reply, probably enthusiastically, that it went great, that it was a brilliant idea to do the interview. And then, she'd turn to Beatrice to get her view. The crucial second opinion. The Prince's eldest daughter was now, in my opinion, the person who could make the difference between us getting the interview and someone else. So, I hastily recalibrated my tactics – less robust, more analytical, less direct, more explanatory, no banter, unless she seemed receptive, I'd keep it sombre until everyone relaxed. I could see Emily and Stew were also a little thrown off, as we all sat down, crammed into that tiny room a few feet from one another, about to try and negotiate the biggest interview of our entire lives.

The six of us sat face to face around the small table. Prince Andrew was to my right, Princess Beatrice was opposite me, in my direct eye line, writing many of our answers down. What followed was an intense two hours of questioning from Prince Andrew and his daughter – and with every minute it became ever clearer that this wasn't won yet.

The meeting veered between everything and nothing. I never even asked who else was in the frame at this point but obviously it was the interview that the whole profession, across the world, would give their right arm to do. The thing that was most surprising was that there was never any *attempt* to find out what we would ask or try to place any conditions on the questions. It was clear that, if the Prince did agree to speak with us, this would be exactly the kind of no holds barred interview that our editorial ethos would demand, and one that our Editor would allow. We worked together to answer everything. This time I didn't worry about dominating the negotiation. I wasn't going to sit back for one second and have a single regret. I was firm in answering whenever I felt I was best placed to do so. I resolved I would get all of my points across, no matter what.

It became clear that Princess Beatrice was very attentive and that Prince Andrew liked my less formal side. I became more congenial. There were some moments of laughter. One second, we'd talk legal matters. The next minute we'd talk about something more personal. I even managed to get in an anecdote about how my mum had once worked for Robert Maxwell!

At one moment, Emily and Stew looked genuinely shocked at how I operate. I go big and I go bold. As we talked, I gave it to Prince Andrew very bluntly. 'Sir. I have lived in this country for over forty years and, until now, I only knew two things about you. It's that you're known as "Air Miles Andy" and "Randy Andy" and I can absolutely tell you that the latter really doesn't help you in your current predicament.' Andrew paused, then laughed. The room collectively exhaled.

For his part, the Prince showed us huge trust. He told us things that are now global knowledge, which no journalist had likely ever heard before. In that tiny room, for the first time, he revealed that he supposedly had an 'alibi'. He told us about Pizza Express. A children's party. He mentioned the sweating, or lack thereof. He talked about how recently he had seen Ghislaine Maxwell. He admitted that he'd made errors of judgement. It was jaw-dropping stuff.

And then, he said something that I will never ever forget. As we concluded things, he turned to Princess Beatrice and said that they had a lot to discuss and they should go, straight after, upstairs, to talk about it, over a cup of tea, with *Mum*. For a split second I almost scoffed; what on earth did a grown man need to talk to his mum for? My brain hadn't connected. And then it hit me. 'Mum' was the Queen. He was saying that he was going to tell her all about it. It was surreal.

When we left, we were all a little breathless. Stew was optimistic that they would say yes, while Emily and I were more circumspect. I am not a superstitious person but, in that moment, it felt like any optimism could jinx things. So, I just kept quiet, and knew we had done absolutely everything we could. Now, we just had to wait to see what decision they would make.

We returned to the office together. Relayed, like a group of drunk teenagers, what had happened to the always calm and collected Esme. She'd, rightly, stayed out of the whole process. Out of every negotiation. Out of every phone call. She kept a cool head for us all. We were going to need it.

We'd agreed to keep the negotiations in a very small circle of trust. It was crucial that other programmes or outlets didn't know how close we were, and we knew that any foolish indiscretion or leak would ruin our chances. If even a diary piece or tweet outed that we were in negotiations, our trust and credibility with the Palace could be trashed. I didn't even tell my mum, my son, my best friend, my boyfriend. It felt strange not to share, but I had promised not to. We told no one else on the team. If we got it, we'd have to bring more people in to get it done. For now, only a handful of us knew.

We found out less than twenty-four hours later. It was the longest twenty-four hours of my life. I couldn't eat. I was a wreck.

We were elated at the news. I cried. With joy, exhaustion and relief. I wouldn't really believe it until those cameras starred rolling. But I wouldn't have to wait long.

By now it was Tuesday 12 November 2019.

In just two days, with virtually no sleep from the combination of excitement and dread, we would all find ourselves back inside Buckingham Palace, face to face with Prince Andrew again, conducting what turned out to be an interview more shocking than any of us could ever have predicted.

11

Prince Andrew: No Sweat

Fifteen feet. That's how far away I am from the back of his chair. I can see the soles of his shoes (hardly scuffed), the back of his head (new haircut), the hem of his trousers (a perfectly judged length) and the nervous tapping of his left foot. The chair itself is befitting of a palace, but it seems a little small for his body.

My own chair is up against the wall of an opulent room larger than most London flats. I'm sitting next to a very friendly woman who, seeing how nervous I was about it all, kindly offered me a martini. Gin, with a twist. I understand Her Majesty is also a fan. It's one of those exchanges that you can hardly believe is happening, chatting idly with someone in Buckingham Palace about your and the monarch's penchant for a cocktail. A Buckingham Palace martini was almost too good to resist, but by now I haven't slept for days, am slightly delirious at the magnitude of it all, and haven't been able to eat, so it wouldn't end well. The charming woman is the Prince's equerry (a sort of royal executive assistant). She's been with him for years and can't speak highly enough of him. She's certain this interview will clear his name – that it's all been a terrible misunderstanding. That, after this, things will go back to normal. I have no idea if she's right. I just want it all done, recorded and in the bag.

Emily Maitlis is in my direct line of vision. Her chair is placed slightly to his left, so I can see all of her. She is nervous, busying herself with her notes, the result of the two days of relentless practice and brainstorms with a small team. Esme has taken the lead. Her calm intellect and methodical nature have been invaluable to us all. She's back at the office, waiting to hear. She can't even discuss it with anyone other than the other Deputy Editor, Verity Murphy, who is now within the circle. This is so huge, so unstable, so easily cancelled, that we still haven't told our other colleagues what we are doing or where we are. If someone asked, I refused to answer. Our families still don't know and it has added to the intensity. Only the Director-General, Tony Hall, and head of News, Fran Unsworth, have been told beyond the team. We are all in it together, for better or worse.

I am, as ever, hot, clutching a bottle of water to prevent coughing – the fear of every TV producer – and trying not to catch anyone's eye. Prince Andrew has his mic fitted, and the camera crews make the final adjustments. Once again, I feel the panic rise within me. We are about to interview a member of the Royal Family about his connections with a sex trafficker. We are about to ask him, on camera, whether he had sex with Virginia Roberts Giuffre, whether he knew about Jeffrey Epstein's terrible acts, and indeed whether he was complicit.

I had arrived early that morning. There's a tiny team of people about to descend – a make-up artist (for Emily and the Prince, if he wants some), an official photographer (though he doesn't know what or who he's photographing) and a second camera crew (one camera on the Prince, one on Emily). I decided to take the bus in, instead of the tube, hoping fresh air would do me some good.

I pass through Kensington, past the golden statue of another Prince, Prince Albert, down through Knightsbridge, on to Hyde Park. I get off next to the statue of Boudicca. She always lifts my spirits. I never came round to the usual TV producer habit of having spare flat shoes in my bag so I'm in my heels again. On the day that Prime Minister Gordon Brown left office, I was once hoisted over a wall (to get to Michael Crick, then

Newsnight political editor) by a police officer when my heels would provide no grip whatsoever. This day, I come a cropper again – Green Park is flooded. I only realise how badly once I start walking across it, and I arrive at the Palace gates with mud splattered all over my boots and down the back of my trousers. Luckily, they're black.

The sea of tourists has no inkling of what we are about to do. I give my name to the security men, but there's a glitch – today we're supposed to enter at the rear of the Palace. And I will need photo identification. For a moment I panic – I'm not sure if I have any on me. Of course, it's not rational – Amanda would tell them to let me in – but, for a moment, I see myself forced to stand outside, alone in the cold, while the interview of my career gets done without me.

Finally, I make it in. I arrive at the same time as the make-up artist. She looks appropriately bemused. As we get taken together through different corridors, into a different lift, up another set of stairs, through cold, sparse hallways, I can see that she's clicked. She whispers, 'Wait, are we interviewing Prince Andrew?' I nod. She says nothing. We traipse along more corridors and finally arrive at the fateful room. It's the south drawing room, apparently. It's full of *Newsnight* clutter. Vast swathes of wooden furniture, gilt chairs, huge green drapes and ceiling details, the marble columns in the doorway contrasting with the modern mess of a television crew. The floor is covered with the activity of making an interview happen – coils of cords unravelling, extra plugs galore. Ugly modern lights on black tripods. The carpet is mostly red, with what looks like flowers or crests, in blue and cream all over it. There are two cameramen, a sound technician, the photographer, Stewart (who is in charge today) and Amanda. There is a small stretch of carpet where Emily and the Prince will sit. Two chairs – upholstered in red, with gold arms and legs and crests on the back of the material – placed opposite one another about ten feet apart, await their guests. Between them is a small wooden table, with two glasses and a bottle of still water. The last hour before an interview starts is stressful and difficult at the best of times. Right now, everyone is the busiest I have ever seen them. Nothing can afford to go wrong.

Emily hasn't arrived yet: she's not late, it just makes sense that a presenter doesn't arrive too early, in case they're left in awkward conversation with a prospective interviewee. Especially one like this. I've set down my bag and am looking to see where I will sit. A row of less ornate chairs line a wall behind where Prince Andrew will sit. That's where I will be. Out of the camera's view, in a row of four people. Amanda is talking to Stewart; Jake, who has produced the film that will run before this interview, mills by the camera crew; there's the equerry and another woman, whom Amanda introduces as her deputy. That's it. No lawyers, no other royal staff, no one. I'd expected a swarm of people to oversee it all. Their absence leads me to wonder how informed other parts of the Palace are about what is taking place here.

In fact, I hadn't met anyone else from the Palace staff during the negotiation. Until now. A tall, white man in his forties or fifties is in the room. He's introduced as 'Communications Secretary to the Queen', I think. We haven't met before. I am told his name is Donal McCabe. His moment in the room is fleeting but, retrospectively, significant. It means several things. First, that the Queen likely knew about the interview (there has been a lot of speculation on that point). Of course, I can't know for certain either way, but, if she didn't, it would be strange to have her member of staff there to come and say 'hello'. I don't recall him asking any questions. He was friendly and professional, spoke to a couple of people in the room and then left. I barely thought about it at the time. Afterwards, it seemed a missed opportunity – if he'd stayed, he would have known the contents of the interview first-hand. Perhaps he would have realised how terribly this would play out for Prince Andrew, for the Palace, for the monarchy. Perhaps they would have had more time to prepare a response. Damage limitation of some kind. As it was, the first time he would have seen it was over forty-eight hours later, when the nation saw it for the first time too.

As I wait for the cameras and lighting to be set up, the equerry tells me that the same room will be used after the interview for Palace 'cinema night'. When we leave, members of the Royal Household will congregate to watch a film, maybe eat popcorn. It will be as if we were never here.

As we chat and I take it all in, Prince Andrew suddenly appears. It's still thirty minutes to go. He introduces himself to the crew, most of whom look uncharacteristically stunned, and then makes his way over to talk to me. It's the norm that, as the producer, you'll have a chat with the interviewee beforehand, share some casual conversation. But I hadn't expected this moment alone with him. He's friendly and chatty – somehow more relaxed than me. I botch the curtsy, doing some kind of weird head bob, combined with crossing my legs, but he doesn't seem to notice or mind. I forget to call him 'Your Royal Highness' initially, and start with 'Sir' so then I throw in a couple of 'Your Royal Highnesses' for good measure. We discuss 'cinema night' and he opens the doors at the end of the room to reveal the projector. As he chats to me about how it works, I'm trying hard to concentrate. To keep him talking. To keep things calm. Turns out that evening they're showing a Renée Zellweger film – *Judy* – have I seen it? 'No, I haven't.' We chat a little about Judy Garland and I think I mention Paxman having a cameo in *Bridget Jones's Diary* but the rest of the conversation passes in a haze. We chat for between five and ten minutes about the room, the weather, the flooded Green Park, and then he moves on to talking to some of the crew, making suggestions about microphones and other technicalities. I survey the scene. It's about twenty minutes to go. Everything is almost in place.

Emily arrives. She's not yet noticed the Prince is already there and she is carrying a number of bags, her hands completely full. In a split second she spots him and real-ises she has no free hand to shake his, and no capacity to curtsy either. So, she hurriedly drops the bags, extends her palm to his, and shakes and bobs (far better than I managed). That's it. We are all here. It's ten minutes to go.

Emily disappears momentarily – I assume to the bath-room – and the air of chaos begins to dissipate. The cameras are all in place and tested, the sound is running, the lights are all firmly fixed, the chairs and table are in position, everyone is ready.

When she gets back, I watch as the crew make final adjustments to her and Prince Andrew's mics. As they test the sound and usher him to the correct chair, the rest of us hurry to take our seats. Stewart stands behind the Prince's chair, to the right of Emily's eye line. Amanda seems to be settling herself next to him, sitting on the floor, a notebook in her hand. There's a collective intake of breath as we all get into position.

Silence. Emily nods. The cameras are rolling. We are off.

'Your Royal Highness, we've come to Buckingham Place in highly unusual circumstances. Normally, we'd be discussing your work, your duty, and we'll come on to that, but today you've chosen to speak out for the first time. Why have you decided to talk now?'

It's the question I get asked the most today. Why did he agree to do this? Why take the enormous risk? It's easy to look back, now that we know how it went, and say that the decision was reckless. But, at the time, it made perfect sense to me, and, clearly, to him and, by extension, to Amanda. Few people think they will do badly, as it happens. Few people imagine their own answers doing them harm. You also have to remember the life he had lived. The third child and second son but always said to be the Queen's favourite. Granted extraordinary access and opportunity. Fawned over wherever he went. The average

CEO, however accomplished or experienced, would have never taken this risk. They would have calculated a hundred reasons not to take the chance. But Andrew had not been subjected to the normal checks and balances. He and his people must have thought this moment, this hour of his life, would change the public perception of him for the better. It seems inconceivable now.

Andrew inhaled before responding. We don't know for sure, but we assumed he had spent the last couple of days in constant rehearsals. Like us, his team must have theorised the questions, decided precisely how to deal with the more serious allegations, considered body language and tone. Deliberated exactly if, or how, he might apologise for the various issues he faced. This first question must have been an obvious one. His first answer would set the tone for the rest of the interview. His face was serious. 'Because there is no good time to talk about Mr Epstein and all things associated, and we've been talking to *Newsnight* for about six months about doing something around the work that I was doing and unfortunately we've just not been able to fit it into either your schedule or my schedule until now. And actually, it's a very good opportunity and I'm delighted to be able to see you today.'

I looked around me. Everyone was waiting to see how he'd fare. We knew our questions; his team knew his answers. How they'd marry would unfold over the minutes ahead.

After that first answer, Emily gave a masterclass in calm, methodical, analytical interviewing. What she had to do was find a line between rigorously pursuing the crucial questions that the nation wanted answered and acting as a conduit for Virginia Roberts Giuffre herself. She held a dual responsibility to the viewer and to his accuser. She couldn't, and didn't, shy away from her central purpose. The answers he gave prove – brilliantly – how effective that thorough, relentless, measured approach can truly be.

The first test would be how, or if, he'd distance himself from Epstein. Emily went straight in. 'As you say, all of this goes back to your friendship with Jeffrey Epstein. How did you first become friends? How did you meet?'

It was crucial to get this right – it's hard to believe he hadn't learned the answer to this verbatim. Prince Andrew gave his account. 'Well, I met through his girlfriend [Ghislaine Maxwell] back in 1999 who . . . and I'd known her since she was at university in the UK and it would be, to some extent, a stretch to say that, as it were, we were close friends. I mean we were friends because of other people and I had a lot of opportunity to go to the United States but I didn't have much time with him. I suppose I saw him once or twice a year, perhaps maybe a maximum of three times a year, and quite often if I was in the United States and doing things and if he wasn't there, he would say, "Well, why don't you come and use my houses?" So I said, "That's very kind, thank you very much indeed." But it would be a considerable stretch to say that he was a very, very close friend. But he had the most extraordinary ability to bring extraordinary people together and that's the bit that I remember as going to the dinner parties where you would meet academics, politicians, people from the United Nations. I mean it was a cosmopolitan group of what I would describe as US eminents.'

His reply was punctuated with pauses and hesitations. But it also encapsulated the unselfconscious tone he took on every question of this kind. I had assumed he would distance himself. Condemn Epstein outright and diminish their shared history. Instead, it sounded like they were close friends, that they knew each other really well and, worse, that Prince Andrew even admired him.

Emily continued, 'You said you weren't very good friends but would you describe him as a good friend, did you trust him?'

I felt sure that he'd carry on and remove himself more from the association but, instead, his answers seemed to flatter Epstein even more and, worse again, flatter himself.

'Yes, I think I probably did but again, I mean I don't go into a friendship looking for the wrong thing, if you understand what I mean. I'm an engaging person, I want to be able to engage, I want to find out, I want to learn, and so you have to remember that I was transitioning out of the Navy at the time and in the transition I wanted to find out more about what was going on, because in the Navy it's a pretty isolated business because you're out at sea the whole time and I was going to become the special representative for international trade and investment. So, I wanted to know more about what was going on in the international business world and so that was another reason for going there. And the opportunities that I had to go to Wall Street and other places to learn whilst I was there were absolutely vital.'

By now, I was exchanging glances with the other team members. We could feel this was not going to go smoothly for His Royal Highness if his answers were all going to be like this. I was sure he'd warm up, do better. Not because I had a hope as to what the outcome would be, but because I knew they'd taken a huge risk, and were expecting a positive return. Clearly, that turned out to be false optimism.

What followed was one astonishing answer after another. Each time I thought it couldn't get any worse, it did. The answers showed first how totally far removed he was from the reality of an average life. 'Am I right in thinking you threw a birthday party for Epstein's girlfriend, Ghislaine Maxwell, at Sandringham?' Emily asked. His correction was my first jaw dropper. 'No, it was a shooting weekend . . . Just a straightforward, a straightforward shooting weekend.' 'A straightforward shooting weekend' went straight to the top of my mental notes, thinking this would be the best line. It didn't stay there for long.

Emily knew this was already a misstep. 'But during these times that he was a guest at Windsor Castle, at Sandringham, the shooting weekend, we now know that he was and had been procuring young girls for sex trafficking.' Prince Andrew knew this answer was important, he needed to get it clear. 'We now know that. At the time there was no indication to me or anybody else that that was what he was doing and certainly when I saw him either in the United States . . . or no, when I saw him in the United States or when I was staying in his houses in the United States, there was no indication, absolutely no indication. And if there was, you have to remember that at the time I was patron of the NSPCC's Full Stop campaign so I was close up with what was going on in those times about getting rid of abuse to children so I knew what the things were to look for, but I never saw them.'

That was probably the best answer he gave. After that the descent downhill continued. Had he been on Epstein's private plane? Yes. Had he stayed on his private island? Yes. Had he stayed at his home in Palm Beach? Yes. Had he visited Ghislaine Maxwell's London home? Yes. Was Epstein at Princess Beatrice's eighteenth birthday party at Windsor Castle? Yes. With each answer, we received a clear sense of his friendship with Maxwell and Epstein. These were not casual acquaintances.

Two months before Epstein attended Beatrice's party, an arrest warrant had been issued for him. The accusation was sexual assault of a minor. Andrew denied he knew anything about it. 'But I mean I'm afraid, you see this is the problem, is that an awful lot of this was going on in the United States and I wasn't a party to it and I knew nothing about it.'

By 2008 Epstein was convicted of soliciting and procuring a minor for prostitution. He was jailed. Andrew said they had no contact during that time. But, Emily knew the killer blow. 'He was released in July. Within months by December of 2010 you went to stay with him at his New York mansion. Why? Why were you staying with a convicted sex offender?'

There are two very famous pictures of Prince Andrew associated with this story. One with Virginia Roberts, aged seventeen, and one with Epstein himself, strolling through a park together. The latter one was during this supposed friendship 'break up'. Andrew knew that looked terrible. 'Right, I have always ... ever since this has happened and since this has become, as it were, public knowledge that I was there, I've questioned myself as to why did I go and what was I doing and was it the right thing to do? Now, I went there with the sole purpose of saying to him that because he had been convicted, it was inappropriate for us to be seen together. And I had a number of people counsel me in both directions, either to go and see him or not to go and see him and I took the judgement call that because this was serious and I felt that doing it over the telephone was the chicken's way of doing it. I had to go and see him and talk to him.'

I was incredulous. Was his explanation going to be that it was the right thing to do to spend time with a convicted sex offender? That it was somehow honourable? 'And I went to see him and I was doing a number of other things in New York at the time and we had an opportunity to go for a walk in the park and that was the conversation coincidentally that was photographed, which was when I said to him, I said, "Look, because of what has happened, I don't think it is appropriate that we should remain in contact," and by mutual agreement during that walk in the park we decided that we would part company and I left, I think it was the next day, and to this day I never had any contact with him from that day forward.'

This interview is now used across the world, by PR and communications professionals and by people in crisis management, as a masterclass in what answers not to give when you're dealing with controversy. That response alone sufficed to show how incapable he was of conveying sympathy, remorse or contrition.

He admitted he was at a dinner party after Epstein's release. He stayed at Epstein's New York mansion. The US literary agent John Brockman said he saw the Prince getting a foot massage from a young woman at the house (he denied it). Emily summed it up. 'It might seem a funny way to break off a friendship, a four-day house party of sorts with a dinner. It's an odd way to break up a friendship.'

Of course, it was a woeful explanation. And yet he wouldn't concede that the whole friendship had been a terrible error of judgement. Emily persisted. 'Do you regret the whole friendship with Epstein?' He should have bitten her hand off for the chance to say, quite simply, yes. Instead, he said, 'Now, still not, and the reason being is that the people I met and the opportunities I was given to learn either by him or because of him were actually very useful.'

I remember having to look down just so I could roll my eyes.

And then, I was shocked all over again. That other photo, the one we have all seen a hundred times, is of Prince Andrew and Virginia Roberts. She says she met him in 2001, that she had dinner with him, danced with him at the infamous Tramp nightclub in London, and then went on to have sex with him in a house in Belgravia belonging to Ghislaine Maxwell. What was his response, Emily asked? His face was rigid. 'I have no recollection of ever meeting this lady, none whatsoever . . . It didn't happen.'

Just like that, he dismissed the entirety of her allegations. The room was silent. You could hear a pin drop. And then, the now notorious alibi was given. 'No, that couldn't have happened because the date that's being suggested I was at home with the children . . . On that particular day that we now understand is the date which is the 10th of March, I was at home, I was with the children and I'd taken Beatrice to a Pizza Express in Woking for a party at, I suppose, sort of four or five in the afternoon. And then because the Duchess was away, we have a simple rule in the family that when one is away the other one is there. I was on terminal leave at the time from the Royal Navy so therefore I was at home.' That was the first time that he'd ever given this reason publicly and it was a bombshell. I knew it would be unforgettable.

Emily went on, 'Why would you remember that so specifically? Why would you remember a Pizza Express birthday and being at home?' The Prince looked resolute in his response. 'Because going to Pizza Express in Woking is an unusual thing for me to do, a very unusual thing for me to do. I've never been . . . I've only been to Woking a couple of times and I remember it weirdly distinctly.'

Just like that, he had given us a panoply of news lines. He denied meeting Virginia Roberts, he didn't drink, he'd never been to the bar in Tramp with her, he'd never bought a drink in fact and, to top it all, in the night in question he'd been at Pizza Express. In Woking. It was news dynamite. And then he gave us even more.

Emily went on. 'She was very specific about that night, she described dancing with you . . . And you profusely sweating and that she went on to have [a] bath possibly.' His answer: 'There's a slight problem with the sweating because I have a peculiar medical condition which is that I don't sweat or I didn't sweat at the time and that was . . . was it . . . yes, I didn't sweat at the time because I had suffered what I would describe as an overdose of adrenaline in the Falkland's War when I was shot at and I simply . . . it was almost impossible for me to sweat. And it's only because I have done a number of things in the recent past that I am starting to be able to do that again. So I'm afraid to say that there's a medical condition that says that I didn't do it so therefore . . .'

It was the answer that launched a thousand memes. Medical experts were called to assess whether this was possible or credible. And that wasn't even the most controversial thing he said. Next? He didn't remember the photo being taken; a discussion of whether it was faked; he had no recollection of meeting Virginia Roberts, or having his hand around her waist in that infamous pose. That, as a royal, he wouldn't have been physically close to someone like that, that he didn't think the casual outfit was something he'd wear in London, that he'd never been upstairs in Ghislaine Maxwell's house (where the photo was supposedly taken). The answers were a journalist's dream. They were also a future defence lawyer's nightmare. I realised, for the first time, that he can't have taken legal advice before speaking to us. These answers, the level of refutation, of detail, were the kind of thing a future prosecutor dreams of.

Emily clarified once more. He didn't recall meeting Virginia Roberts. He denied having sex with her. He didn't have any kind of sexual contact with her?

His responses carried the unavoidable implication that Virginia had made the whole thing up. 'Are you saying you don't believe her, she's lying?' His response was opaque. 'That's a very difficult thing to answer because I'm not in a position to know what she's trying to achieve, but I can tell you categorically I don't remember meeting her at all. I do not remember a photograph being taken and I've said consistently and frequently that we never had any sort of sexual contact whatever.'

He should have stopped there, but he didn't. His next response stayed with me. Everyone else remembers the sweat, the Pizza Express, but I couldn't get over this next bit. Emily carried on her methodical questioning. 'For the record, is there any way you could have had sex with that young woman or any young woman trafficked by Jeffrey Epstein in any of his residences?'

Andrew repeated his denials. 'No, and without putting too fine a point on it, if you're a man it is a positive act to have sex with somebody. You have to take some sort of positive action and so therefore if you try to forget, it's very difficult to try and forget a positive action and I do not remember anything. I can't, I've wracked my brain and thinking oh . . . when the first allegations, when the allegations came out originally I went, well, that's a bit strange, I don't remember this and then I've been through it and through it and through it over and over and over again and no, nothing. It just never happened.'

He had wracked his brain for a 'positive action'? Was
this a royal euphemism for penetration? It just got worse
and worse. Next he tried to say that he wouldn't have
necessarily noticed what was going on because of his
royal status. 'The other aspect of this is that . . . is that I
live in an institution at Buckingham Palace which has
members of staff walking around all the time, and I don't
wish to appear grand but there were a lot of people who
were walking around Jeffrey Epstein's house. As far as I
was aware, they were staff, they were people that were
working for him, doing things, I . . . as it were, I interacted
with them, if you will, to say good morning, good afternoon, but I didn't, if you see what I mean, interact with
them in a way that was, you know, what are you doing
here, why are you here, what's going on?'

It was quite something to say that he might not have
noticed that his close-ish friend was surrounded by young
women because he was used to having lots of staff at
Buckingham Palace. Emily didn't let it go. 'But you'd
notice if there were hundreds of underage girls in
Buckingham Palace, wouldn't you?' He denied that had
happened while he was Epstein's guest. 'Oh God, but
sorry you would notice if there were hundreds of underage girls in Jeffrey's house. Wasn't there, not when I was
there. Now he may have changed his behaviour patterns

in order for that not to be obvious to me, so I don't . . . I mean this is . . . you're asking me to speculate on things that I just don't know about.'

It was a total fiasco. None of it made sense. He'd still not expressed any real regret about the friendship, he'd still not expressed any real horror about the allegations of the crimes, and, to top it all, he'd basically called Virginia Roberts a liar. As a journalist, as a lawyer, as a human, I couldn't believe how poorly judged the answers were.

The next exchange launched a debate about what he had, or hadn't, done over the years to assist in any of the investigations. 'You seem utterly convinced you're telling the truth, would you be willing to testify or give a statement under oath if you were asked?' He replied, 'Well, I'm like everybody else and I will have to take all the legal advice that there was before I was to do that sort of thing. But if push came to shove and the legal advice was to do so, then I would be duty bound to do so.'

What about the FBI, would he talk to them? He repeated his response. 'Again, I'm bound by what my legal advice is . . . legal advisers tell me.' Their advice was clearly to say nothing to these agencies. But, in this interview, he'd said so, so much. The two positions seemed irreconcilable. That's why I felt sure they hadn't been consulted. If I was right, it was a shocking risk to take.

He deferred to the coroner on whether Epstein had committed suicide. And refused to be drawn in to commenting on Ghislaine Maxwell. 'If there are questions that Ghislaine has to answer, that's her problem, I'm afraid, I'm not in a position to be able to comment one way or the other.' But then he admitted he'd seen her earlier this year, in the spring or summer of 2019. He seemed momentarily confused on whether it was before Epstein had been arrested, and then decided it was after. Apparently they didn't discuss him.

Had the whole episode been damaging to the Queen? 'I don't believe it's been damaging to the Queen at all. It has to me and it's been a constant drip, if you see what I mean, in the background that people want to know. If I was in a position to be able to answer all these questions in a way that gave sensible answers other than the ones that I have given that gave closure then I'd love it but I'm afraid I can't. I'm just not in a position to do so because I'm just as much in the dark as many people.'

Time was running out, there was still no fulsome regret. Sensing we were close to the end, Emily gave him one more chance, an opportunity to rue the relationship. 'I wonder if you have any sense now of guilt, regret or shame about any of your behaviour and your friendship with Epstein?' She handed it to him on a plate. Surely he'd finally take this, his last chance, to clarify that it had all been a terrible mistake?

I looked up from the floor, watched him gather himself for one of the final answers. 'As far as Mr Epstein is concerned, it was the wrong decision to go and see him in 2010. As far as my association with him was concerned, it had some seriously beneficial outcomes in areas that have nothing and have nothing to do with what I would describe as what we're talking about today.' It was extraordinary that he couldn't see how terrible that sounded. 'On balance, could I have avoided ever meeting him? Probably not and that's because of my friendship with Ghislaine, it was . . . it was . . . it was inevitable that we would have come across each other. Do I regret the fact that he has quite obviously conducted himself in a manner unbecoming? Yes.'

For the first time Emily almost snapped. 'Unbecoming? He was a sex offender.' The room went quiet. All sides knew it was an awful thing for him to have said, even Prince Andrew. 'Yeah, I'm sorry, I'm being polite, I mean in the sense that he was a sex offender. But no, was I right in having him as a friend? At the time, bearing in mind this was some years before he was accused of being a sex offender. I don't think there was anything wrong then, the problem was the fact that once he had been convicted . . .

I stayed with him and that's . . . that's . . . that's the bit that . . . that . . . that, as it were, I kick myself for on a daily basis because it was not something that was becoming of a member of the Royal Family and we try and uphold the highest standards and practices and I let the side down, simple as that.'

That was his final position? That he had let the side down by the act of staying with Epstein after all that had happened? It was quite a position to take. It was to be his penultimate answer.

Emily asked her final question. 'This interview has been exceptionally rare, you might not speak on this subject again, is there anything you feel has been left unsaid that you would like to say now?' A message of regret for the terrible acts his 'friend' had committed perhaps? Andrew's chance ebbed away.

'No, I don't think so. I think you've probably dragged out most of what is required and I'm truly grateful for the opportunity that you've given me to be able to discuss this with you.'

'Your Royal Highness, thank you.'

That was it. It was over.

The cameras stopped rolling. I couldn't look at anyone. I was still processing his answers, the words he had used, the soon-to-be-unforgettable sound bites. I could barely believe his people hadn't stopped the interview. I would have, despite the consequences.

As mics were removed, Stewart chatted with Amanda Thirsk, who had remained silent on the floor throughout, only once tugging at Stewart's trouser leg. Did she realise how damaging it had been? Did he realise how good it was? The equerry was gathering herself next to me. I couldn't gauge her reaction but I find it hard to be fake, so I worded my first question to her carefully. 'How did you think it went?' She beamed back at me. 'Wasn't he wonderful!' she said, smiling. In one way, she was right. 'Yes, yes, he was,' I replied.

I'd expected Amanda to be distraught, the Prince to look shaken or concerned, but he seemed ebullient. She was smiling. Who knows if it was a genuine smile or forced by circumstance but, ever the professional, she showed no palpable reaction. And then it hit me: he *actually* thought it had gone well. In fact, he was in fine spirits. He was in such a good mood that he offered us all a tour of the Palace. I couldn't go. I wouldn't be able to speak to him in good faith. Of course, Emily couldn't decline. I don't know how she kept her composure.

As the two of them left the room, I caught Stewart's eye. As the Deputy Editor he knew full well what had just happened. As producers, this is the moment when you desperately want the material out of the building and safely back at HQ. As the camera and lighting crews started to dismantle their equipment – on a bit of a deadline because of that cinema night – Jake Morris held the small, insignificant-looking recording drives in his hands. They were the most precious recordings any of us had ever had. We all felt a mutual sense of urgency to get them back immediately.

Leaving was a blur. I felt a mild sense of panic that the recording would all be accidentally erased, that it could drop and smash into bits, that somehow it wouldn't make it to air. We scrambled into a black cab, high on adrenaline.

We had two days between the recording and the one-hour special on Saturday night. I could barely believe the Palace would let it go ahead. Surely there would be some kind of legal intervention? Surely they'd try and spike it, once they had a moment to realise how hideously badly it had gone? Surely Esme would face legal threats beforehand? The Director-General would be involved?

Nothing and nobody came. Our entire recording, barring a couple of answers about the Prince's charitable works, made it to air. It would be forty-five minutes of television history.

12

Prince Andrew: Aftershock

Thursday 14 November was the last evening of calm. Finally, we told our colleagues what was happening (stunned). I told my mum (proud), my best friend Yalda Hakim (excited), my boyfriend Tom (speechless) and my son Lucas ('Who is Prince Andrew?').

The next day, we tweeted the first hints of what we had. A solitary photo – the iconic image of Emily and Andrew, side view, seated face to face – and these words: 'WORLD EXCLUSIVE: In a #Newsnight @BBCTwo interview recorded yesterday at Buckingham Palace, Emily Maitlis talks to Prince Andrew about his relationship with Jeffrey Epstein – the first time he's answered questions on the scandal.'

And there, underneath it all, my Editor Esme Wren wrote the tweet that changed my life. 'Full credit to our indefatigable interview producer @SamMcAlister1 for securing this world exclusive . . .'

And then all hell broke loose.

Calls poured in. Producers from all over the building streamed into the office. All the papers got in touch. All the other TV channels too. It was the interview everyone had wanted. But only we had it.

That period of time was a total blur. Stewart was still doing the final edits and the programme was twenty-four hours away. It wasn't going to be aired within the usual *Newsnight* programme at 10.30 p.m. It was too important. We would do one tantalising preview clip on the Friday programme and air the entire clip in the primetime slot of 9 p.m. on Saturday 16 November on BBC Two.

I spent those twenty-four hours wandering around, hoping the interview wouldn't be thwarted. I busied myself with looking after my son and then, on that Saturday evening, went to Tom's place to watch the whole interview, just like so many people across the country, from the comfort of a sofa. As I'd been sitting behind Prince Andrew throughout, it was a complete revelation to see him, full face on, with the various facial expressions and contortions that the interview revealed. After the first answer, I couldn't sit still. I stood, mouth open, in front of the screen. For the whole hour I remained there, enraptured. Each time he answered, we both gasped. Of course, I had heard it all before, but seeing it like this, alongside the nation, was somehow more shocking. Until then, only a handful of us knew what had happened. From that moment the whole country, the whole world, knew.

Social media went crazy, the papers printed page after page of analysis, the interview was subtitled and discussed across the globe. Everyone agreed on one thing: it had been an unmitigated disaster for Prince Andrew.

I can only imagine the slow unfolding of the drama for Amanda Thirsk and the Prince. The papers asked why on earth they had agreed to do this, who had made it happen, who had made the terrible error of letting him take part. At that stage, our two lives parted ways – the *Daily Mail* (which has done an article on the Prince virtually every day since) tracked me down. They did a whole page on us both, entitled 'The women who made it happen'. They included pictures of us. It read, 'Credit is due to *Newsnight* for landing the interview, but in particular to Samantha McAlister, a former barrister turned TV producer.' They had clearly read my LinkedIn profile, which contained some facts about my past that seemed rather incongruent in the circumstances: 'She is a former European Debating Champion and her silky persuasive skills were invaluable in negotiations with the Palace.' Silky persuasive skills! I was so used to being a background member of the team and now my phone was on fire. Messages from all across the world, from friends, colleagues, people in the media asking me to do interviews, features, photo shoots. It was overwhelming. The *Guardian* ran an article on the Sunday: 'Who were the main players behind the Prince Andrew interview?' My photo was emblazoned across it all, my description below: 'A BBC journalist since 2003, she joined *Newsnight* in 2011, where she is prized for her ability to secure hard-to-get interviews.'

I appreciated being mentioned. Too often producers in our industry were nameless when their hard work came to fruition. Too often the impression would be given that a story or interview had somehow miraculously 'happened' without explanation. So many of us were worn down by credit being given to other people, more senior or more high profile. But, this time, that didn't happen.

That night I still didn't sleep. The adrenaline hadn't left me.

Throughout the night, the messages kept coming. As morning arrived, the calls started up again. News networks. Papers. A call from Sir Philip Green (who I had been fruitlessly chasing for an interview for years) – to congratulate me, but also to say how delighted he was that he'd previously declined speaking to us. I didn't open the curtains. A neighbour texted, said he thought he'd seen cameras outside. My heart was racing. It wasn't an attention I was used to. My son was at his dad's place and so I lay there, hour after hour, fielding messages and calls. I didn't eat, I didn't wash, I didn't leave the house. It was light, then it was dark. That was my day.

The next day, Monday, I had to go to work as normal. There was a deluge of emails congratulating us, from the great and the good, the Director-General Tony Hall, the Controller of BBC Two Patrick Holland. Two people I had never spoken to before. The head of our department, Jo Carr, came in person. She told me off when I tried to share the credit with others. 'Own it! You did it!' she said. I appreciated her kind words but didn't want to put other noses out of joint. Credit is a tricky issue. Others had worked with me and borne the strain too. I wanted to make sure everyone got mentioned every time – after all, there was enough credit to go around for everyone. Stew, who'd been such a cool-headed Deputy Editor and exec; Jake Morris, who'd spent so many hours on research for the opening introductory film; Alicia Queiro, who had worked on production back in the office; Kate Moore, who had achieved wonders on the logistics. And others who'd contributed their man and woman hours to help.

Meanwhile, the papers lambasted Amanda Thirsk. Ridiculed her for 'letting' the Prince do the interview. The way she was being hounded profoundly disturbed me. What she had done was believe in her boss – his own answers had landed him in hot water. I felt strangely protective towards her – she had spoken to me for months, trusted us with this opportunity, and now her professional life lay in tatters. I wanted to message her but Stew, as Deputy Editor, thought everything should go through him because it was such a sensitive situation. I understood his logic but felt shitty not messaging her to say I hoped she was as OK as she could be in the circumstances. As a producer, I knew she'd likely be the one to take the fall for this. No doubt, by now, she knew it too.

Of course, it was right that Prince Andrew was criticised, that he faced reproach for all of his actions, for his inadequate answers, but I carried a feeling of responsibility towards Amanda that I couldn't shake. It wasn't the same for other people on the team – they'd met her for moments, or hours, but I had been communicating with her for many months. We were both single parents (she had lost her husband, I had divorced mine), doing our jobs to the best of our abilities. I respected her and I knew she respected me.

By Wednesday, I was starting to crash. I worked a three-day week – my entire career at *Newsnight* had been part-time – but that week, those three days felt like forever. Finally, on Wednesday night, I dragged myself home. Slumped on the sofa. Lucas sat on the other one. Some cats wandered in and out. Finally, I felt calm. Not for long.

On Wednesday 20 November, a statement was released from Prince Andrew, Duke of York. I heard it first as I watched the news, live, from my sofa.

It has become clear to me over the last few days that the circumstances relating to my former association with Jeffrey Epstein has become a major disruption to my family's work and the valuable work going on in the many organisations and charities that I am proud to support.

My heart was in my throat.

Therefore, I have asked Her Majesty if I may step back from public duties for the foreseeable future, and she has given her permission.

I continue to unequivocally regret my ill-judged association with Jeffrey Epstein. His suicide has left many unanswered questions, particularly for his victims, and I deeply sympathise with everyone who has been affected and wants some form of closure. I can only hope that, in time, they will be able to rebuild their lives. Of course, I am willing to help any appropriate law enforcement agency with their investigations, if required.

At last, the apology to the victims had come. A member of the Royal Family was stepping back from public life. He was no longer who he had been a week earlier. It was, to use the word correctly, unprecedented. I felt a combination of panic and fear. Perhaps it would have been easier if I were in the office. With colleagues around me. But, on that sofa, uneasiness set in. I am not a paranoid person but, for the next few days, that was my prevailing feeling. There was no threat to me. No one ever sent me any cruel messages or even abusive tweets. But I felt alone and vulnerable.

The media interest over those days was intense. The story led the front pages of papers all across the world. If I had a pound for every time the *Daily Mail* had mentioned it since, I'd be a billionaire. Ant and Dec talked about it (the true mark of societal impact). A thousand memes were launched. A million jokes about Pizza Express and 'no sweat' were shared. Just like that, what we had done, and what he had said, passed into the lexicon of the nation. It was the other legacy of the interview.

Amanda Thirsk also stepped back from her role and then eventually left. I ignored Stewart's direction and messaged her. Offered to meet if she was so inclined. Meanwhile, we carried on. There were award ceremonies. I met with Tony Hall, the Director-General, to discuss it all. He'd been involved in that other huge BBC interview, with Princess Diana and Martin Bashir. Everyone was saying it was the biggest thing the Corporation had done since. Tony was congenial and chatty. Of course, with the benefit of hindsight, there are things I wished I had asked him. But his reputation wasn't tarnished back then. I messaged Martin Bashir too – thought it would be interesting to meet, compare experiences, discuss our negotiations, how it had all happened. He said he was 'too busy'. Now, I can see why.

The Royal Family was shaken by all that happened. And new controversies arose. The *Mail* reported that Princess Beatrice had been at the negotiation. Someone must have leaked it. I felt sick for her. Tried to work out who had done it. No one else seemed to care and we never did find out.

Next, Prince Harry and Meghan Markle announced their departure from their royal roles. People discussed whether Andrew's interview had been the final straw. The rift between the brothers, William and Harry, deepened in full view.

Then there was the worry about the Queen's health.

Then, Covid hit. We all know how that went. I caught it early, in March 2020, just after an awards ceremony. It was what we'd now consider a 'superspreader' event. Within days I was overcome by fever and pain. I couldn't eat, walk, talk. I deteriorated fast into a state of near constant delirium. Only poor Lucas was with me in the house – in another room, with no food. Piers Morgan kindly mentioned I was sick on air and suddenly offers of shopping came in – Sam Washington, the Sky News presenter, dropped off bags of stuff for Lucas, so did Claudia-Liza Vanderpuije from Channel 5. I couldn't even properly thank them. Trudging up and down the stairs was almost impossible. I had to crawl to the bathroom. Lucas survived on god knows what. I ate only a carrot a day. It took four months before I could make it further than the end of the street. My doctor said I might never work again – in that state I certainly would not have been able to. I was genuinely grateful to be alive.

During that time, the interview felt a world away. I knew that Ghislaine Maxwell had been arrested. The volume of accusations against her increased. That Prince Andrew was likely to be further implicated. But I wasn't fully conscious of it all. I didn't start working again until September 2020. We muddled through home schooling.

I found it hard to concentrate. Slowly, my strength and mental acuity were restored, and I began to feel more like myself. By then, Prince Andrew was still out of public life, and Maxwell was facing eight charges relating to grooming underage girls for Epstein between 1994 and 2004. His fate and hers were irrevocably linked. Calls for him to 'co-operate' with the FBI grew louder. His representatives insisted he had done what he had been asked. A legal and media war of words was under way.

By November I was just about back to working properly. And then, just before the twenty-fifth anniversary of Martin Bashir's interview with Princess Diana, the controversy around the circumstances in which that interview had been secured came back, full throttle, into the news. Earl Spencer, who I had stayed in touch with sporadically, went public again with his allegations against Bashir and the BBC. The interview, he said, had been procured by Martin Bashir by a litany of lies. That Diana had been convinced by him that the Prince of Wales's staff had launched a campaign against her. He said Diana had only agreed to the interview under the belief that what Bashir said was true. That she would never have agreed to do it otherwise. Bank statements had been forged. Earl Spencer was, understandably, furious. He wanted answers. Lord Dyson was appointed to conduct a review. By now Lord

Hall had left and taken up a new role at the National Gallery. Tim Davie, the new Director-General, said the BBC was determined to find out what had happened. The scandal engulfed the nation. Now, it was Bashir's behaviour, our collective behaviour, that dominated the front pages. The more I learned about the allegations, the more appalled I was. A graphic designer who had blown the whistle had lost his job. It seemed clear there had been some kind of cover-up. All I could feel was betrayal and anger.

While the report gathered its evidence, I came to an important conclusion. I wanted to leave the BBC.

EPILOGUE

The BBC gave me access to important, inspiring and complex public figures. In addition to the stories you've read here, I also worked on interviews with Sheryl Sandberg, President Clinton, Prime Minister Netanyahu, Rachel Dolezal, Prime Minister Trudeau and Trevor Noah, among others. These were unforgettable experiences that allowed me to peer into worlds – politics, celebrity, technology, big business – I would have never otherwise known.

But nothing lasts forever. During my years at the BBC, I felt it had become less editorially robust and less impartial (despite much internal pushback) and this was not something I was comfortable with, though it has been a general trend for many outlets. As I fell out of step with the prevailing view, I decided I didn't want to continually be a dissenting voice.

I had hoped that, following the success of the Prince Andrew interview, greater opportunities might arise for me. I asked for a pay rise, and it was denied. I asked for a bonus, but they were no longer allowed. I asked for a promotion, and that wasn't possible either. I wanted to do public events, and that wasn't permitted. I had invitations to feature in various magazines and newspapers but was restricted to one small interview for GQ, and nothing more. When we won awards, I never got to speak, or to keep any of the awards themselves, so I would pay for my own replicas! Perhaps I would not have been permitted to write this book, despite swathes of books, sometimes contentious, from presenters and correspondents across the organisation. The BBC had no way to accommodate a producer in my position. And I didn't want to end up feeling bitter when there had been so much to love throughout my career.

And so, when the opportunity arose to apply for voluntary redundancy, I took it. It was turned down the first time (I was still deemed 'business essential') but I got there in the end.

Before I left, I finally got to see Amanda Thirsk. She was nothing but gracious and wished me the best. We are still in touch from time to time.

As with many relationships, there is an element of relief when it ends, and other emotions besides. I was relieved that I didn't have to deal with the circus surrounding Martin Bashir (that he lost the clothes of the murdered nine-year-old Karen Hadaway seventeen years after swearing he didn't remember being given them by her mother). And it felt good to say whatever I wanted without worrying.

In the same month that I left (October 2021) something very vindicating happened – I got a call from Katie Bailiff, CEO of Women in Film and Television UK. She told me that Emily and I had won the BBC News and Factual Award for the Prince Andrew interview. She said that the WFTV judges wanted to recognise the special and important role that producers have in making historic events like this happen. I would get an award of my own and would get the chance to make a speech.

I finally got to articulate something that I had felt so strongly during my entire career, something that really mattered to me: publicly praise producers everywhere. A lot is expected of a producer – in news, factual, film and scripted TV – and they can be the main reason a show happens, from conception of an idea to its execution. But they are largely invisible. And unlike with films or TV shows, with their big-name producers who often attract the talent, there is not a lot of cachet in the role, even at a place like the BBC. So, I was delighted with an award for my work but more thrilled that someone like me could even get an award.

The speech got 80,000 views, so not exactly Kardashian levels but clearly it struck a chord. Producers are just one of many background figures in the media. So, this book is for them and many others who work their arses off and are often overlooked, underpaid, unappreciated. They tend to be dedicated, smart and hard-working people. And they matter.

Acknowledgements

To everyone who kindly told me I should write a book, I listened!

To my lovely literary agent, Sarah Ballard, who believed in me right from the start, even though I'd never written a book before (no biggie . . .).

Cecilia Stein, who edited my words with patience, skill and good humour throughout.

Tom Lane, who never wavered in his support for me, and helped me laugh and martini my way through the whole experience.

Yalda Hakim, whose friendship and kindness has been the backbone of many of my life decisions, and who is the only person who loves scones as much as I do.

Megan Murphy, who told me I could do this all the way through, and whose counsel was invaluable as we walked for miles and supped coffees and laughed like banshees.

To Lucas, who endured all the tap-tap-tapping away at the computer, and was my partner in crime and inspiration (from the other sofa) throughout.

To all the interviewees who put their faith and trust in us to tell their stories.

And to my friends at *Newsnight* – in particular Esme, Stewart and Emily – who were my team for a decade, and with whom I had the best of times.